Jump Into Math

Strategies to Help Students Succeed with Computation

Grade 3

by
Barry Doran, EdS
Leland Graham, PhD

Carson-Dellosa Publishing Company, Inc.
Greensboro, North Carolina

This book has been correlated to state, national, and Canadian provincial standards. Visit *www.carsondellosa.com* to search for and view its correlations to your standards.

Editors: Carrie Fox, Beki Benning, and Susan Morris

Layout Design: Lori Jackson

Inside Illustrations: Jenny Campbell

Cover Design: Lori Jackson and Peggy Jackson

ISBN: 978-1-60022-094-4

Table of Contents

Skills Index

Introducing *Jump Into Math*

• A DIAGNOSTIC GUIDE •

Jump Into Math is designed to provide practical suggestions for overcoming common stumbling blocks students encounter with computational skills. Often, teachers have difficulty planning a meaningful and successful corrective instructional program for learners who are having trouble with computational skills. *Jump Into Math* is a ready-to-use program of study for these struggling learners that offers a systematic analysis of troublesome concepts, step-by-step instruction for teachers, and meaningful practice for students.

Overview

The development of computational skills is a major component of any mathematics program. Computation is included in the Numbers and Operations strand as outlined by The National Council of Teachers of Mathematics in their *Principles and Standards for School Mathematics* (2000). The NCTM Standards advocate computational fluency for students and further suggest that students who are able to compute efficiently and accurately can significantly increase their scores on standardized tests and build a sturdy foundation for success with higher math, such as algebra. Poor computation skills are a significant handicap to many mathematics students. Therefore, a comprehensive diagnosis of students' errors and misconceptions in arithmetic, followed by corrective instruction and focused practice, is essential.

Computational errors are not always the result of carelessness or improper procedures. Teachers sometimes have the misconception that "practice makes perfect," but perfection comes with improvement over time. If students practice the same mistakes over and over again, improvement will be slow or will not happen at all. For a student to improve and reach "perfection," the "practice" must be accompanied by carefully planned developmental instruction that is designed to help students overcome their specific problems.

Careful observations of students at work and an analysis of their written work are key components of meaningful instruction. There are four general categories of errors in computation: wrong operation, fact errors, defective algorithms, and random responses (guessing). Most student errors can be eliminated if they have a thorough understanding of the procedures used to perform a computation. This requires the student to experience hands-on practice with the underlying skills and concepts. Teachers must plan a developmental sequence of skills that provides the struggling learner with success-oriented experiences that eliminate frustration and failure.

The following page will explain *Jump Into Math*'s developmental approach to encouraging students' computational fluency.

How to Use *Jump Into Math*

Each grade-level book in the *Jump Into Math* series is divided into specific number and computational skills. Each section includes a diagnostic test with teacher notes, teaching activities, and student activities targeted to specific items on the test. In addition, a comprehensive test is included at the end of the book. The components of the *Jump Into Math* program are described below.

Diagnostic Tests—The diagnostic tests target the fundamental concepts of each skill. The tests are illustrative and can be modified by the teacher to meet individual program requirements. The intent is to provide an example of how diagnostic tests can be used to analyze students' errors. Some teachers will want to use the tests in order. Others may want to begin with Part II or Part III then, based on students' scores, either drop back to Part I or move on to other parts. The diagnostic tests may also be used to quickly determine placement of new students who enroll during the school year.

Teacher Notes and Teaching Activities—Following each diagnostic test is an analysis of each part of the test that references the specific skills addressed in each test item. The teacher notes have been designed to provide information about potential problem areas for students. Sample teaching strategies, activities, sample problems, and suggestions for follow-up instruction are included.

Student Activities—Student activities for practice are included for each problem type on the diagnostic tests. These activities provide practice of the skills, remediation, reteaching, extension to related skills, and maintenance of skills (review). Each practice page is correlated to a specific test item.

Comprehensive Test—At the end of the book, there is a multiple-choice test that includes items covering all of the computational skills appropriate to the grade level.

Diagnostic Test: Numeration

Directions: Write your answer to each question in the space provided.

Part I: Place Value to the Thousands Period

1. What digit is in the hundreds place?

    2,573

    _____

2. What is the place value of the underlined digit?

    23,456

    _____

3. Write the number four thousand three hundred twenty-one.

    _____

4. What is the value of the underlined digit?

    37,250

    _____

5. Write the number sixteen thousand two hundred thirty-five.

    _____

6. Write 3,485 in expanded form.

    _____ + _____ + _____ + _____

7. Write 2,000 + 100 + 40 + 3 in standard form.

_____

9. Write 13,876 in expanded form.

_____ + _____ + _____

+ _____ + ____

8. Write 30 + 400 + 8 + 4,000 in standard form.

_____

10. Write 20,000 + 300 + 4,000 + 8 in standard form.

_____

TEACHER ASSESSMENT AREA

Directions: Shade the boxes that correspond to correct test items.

Skill		Item Number				
Place Value		1	2	3	4	5
Expanded Notation		6	7	8	9	10

TOTAL CORRECT: _____

CD-104225 • Jump Into Math • © Carson-Dellosa

Teacher Notes and Activities

NUMERATION PART I: PLACE VALUE TO THE THOUSANDS PERIOD

TEACHER NOTES: Place Value
(Diagnostic Test Part I: Test Items 1–5)

Students have had extensive practice with place values from the ones period: hundreds, tens, and ones. Now, introduce the thousands period: hundred-thousands, ten-thousands, and one-thousands.

THOUSANDS			ONES		
Hundreds	Tens	Ones	Hundreds	Tens	Ones
		3	4	6	1

To organize numbers and make them easier to read, digits are arranged in periods, or sets, separated by commas. For example, the place value chart above shows the number **3,461**. The digit **3** is in the thousands period and is separated from the digits **4**, **6**, and **1** in the ones period. In words, the number is read, "three thousand four hundred sixty-one."

TEACHING ACTIVITY: "Modeling Thousands" (Place Value)

Use an overhead projector and base ten blocks to demonstrate numbers in the thousands. Show the following example:

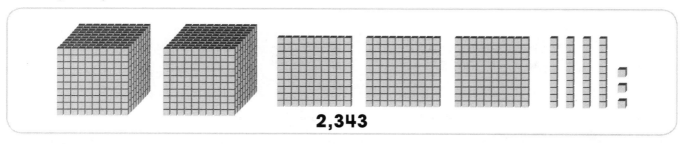

2,343

Give each student a place value mat with the charts as shown below. Instruct students to model numbers on their mats using base ten blocks.

THOUSANDS			ONES		
Hundreds	Tens	Ones	Hundreds	Tens	Ones

Give students the following numbers to model: **1,342   8,234   3,421   2,540**

TEACHER NOTES: Expanded Notation

(Diagnostic Test Part I: Test Items 6–10)

Students should be able to write large numbers in both standard form and expanded form, and by using digits as well as number words.

TEACHING ACTIVITY: "Charting Thousands" (Expanded Notation)

Demonstrate different ways to show numbers on an overhead projector or chalkboard.

Use base ten blocks to model **1,430**.

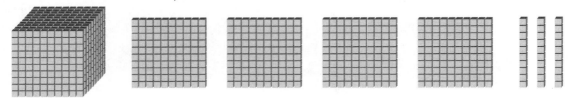

Write the number in expanded form: **1,000 + 400 + 30**.

Write the number in standard form: **1,430**

Write the number in words: **one thousand four hundred thirty***

Ask students to practice with charts like the one below.
*Note: Remind students that number words for numbers in the tens and ones places combined must be hyphenated if the number is not a multiple of ten. (See *forty-three* and *thirty-six* in the chart below.)

MODEL	EXPANDED FORM	STANDARD FORM	NUMBER WORD
	1,000 + 100 + 40 + 3	1,143	One thousand one hundred forty-three
	2,000 + 200 + 30 + 6	2,236	Two thousand two hundred thirty-six

The Model Shows

Place Value to the Thousands Period

Test Items 1–5

Directions: Use base ten blocks to model the numbers. Then, write the numbers in the place value charts.

Example:
The place value chart shows the number **3,461**. A comma separates the ones and thousands periods. In words, the number is read: three thousand four hundred sixty-one.

THOUSANDS				ONES		
Hundreds	Tens	Ones		Hundreds	Tens	Ones
		3	,	4	6	1

1. 3,542

THOUSANDS			ONES		
Hundreds	Tens	Ones	Hundreds	Tens	Ones

2. 8,654

THOUSANDS			ONES		
Hundreds	Tens	Ones	Hundreds	Tens	Ones

3. 5,781

THOUSANDS			ONES		
Hundreds	Tens	Ones	Hundreds	Tens	Ones

4. 21,567

THOUSANDS			ONES		
Hundreds	Tens	Ones	Hundreds	Tens	Ones

5. 17,834

THOUSANDS			ONES		
Hundreds	Tens	Ones	Hundreds	Tens	Ones

6. 33,603

THOUSANDS			ONES		
Hundreds	Tens	Ones	Hundreds	Tens	Ones

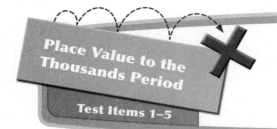

Place Value to
the Thousands

Directions: For each number below, write the place value of the underlined digit.

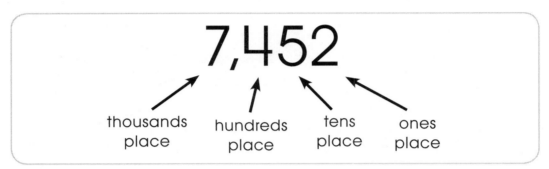

7,452

thousands place   hundreds place   tens place   ones place

1. 1,4̲63 _____

2. 7̲,535 _____

3. 3,81̲9̲ _____

4. 4,34̲7 _____

5. 5̲,425 _____

6. 9,3̲09 _____

7. 2,97̲4 _____

8. 6,95̲0̲ _____

Directions: Write the digit in each place named below.

9. 3,409 _____ hundreds

10. 2,274 _____ ones

11. 7,921 _____ thousands

12. 9,553 _____ hundreds

13. 5,862 _____ tens

14. 4,386 _____ thousands

Number Names

Place Value to the Thousands Period

Test Items 1–5

Directions: Study the example below. On the lines provided, write the number words in standard form.

Example: four thousand nine hundred forty-two = 4,942

1. seven hundred forty-five

   _____

2. eight thousand ninety

   _____

3. five thousand two hundred twenty-two

   _____

4. thirty-seven thousand two hundred fifty-one

   _____

5. fourteen thousand five hundred thirty-four

   _____

6. eighteen thousand five hundred four

   _____

7. twenty-three thousand seven hundred sixteen

   _____

8. ten thousand eight hundred seventy

   _____

9. eighty-one thousand three hundred ninety-three

   _____

10. fifty thousand six hundred forty-one

   _____

Expanded Notation

Test Items 6–10

Working with Models

Directions: Study the example below. Then, write the expanded form of each modeled number.

Example:

The number in expanded form: **1,000 + 300 + 40**

1.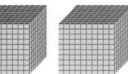

The number in expanded form: _____

2.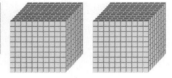

The number in expanded form: _____

3.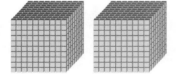

The number in expanded form: _____

4.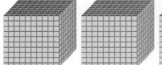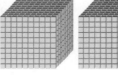

The number in expanded form: _____

Numbers in Many Forms

Expanded Notation

Test Items 6–10

Directions: Complete the worksheet below for each model.

> **Example:**
>
>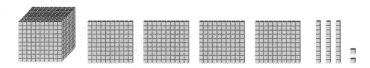
>
> Write the number in expanded form: **1,000 + 400 + 30 + 2**
> Write the number in standard form: **1,432**
> Write the number word: **one thousand four hundred thirty-two**

MODEL	EXPANDED FORM	STANDARD FORM	NUMBER WORD
1.			
2.			
3.			

Expanded Notation

Test Items 6–10

Mixing It Up

Directions: Study the example below. Then, write each number in standard form or expanded form.

> **Example:**
> Standard form : **7,331**
> Expanded form : **7,000 + 300 + 30 + 1**

1. Write 9,763 in expanded form. _____ + _____ + _____ + _____

2. Write 8,175 in expanded form. _____ + _____ + _____ + _____

3. Write 10,000 + 5,000 + 400 + 70 + 8 in standard form. _____

4. Write 20,000 + 1,000 + 600 + 90 + 9 in standard form. _____

5. Write 10,866 in expanded form. _____ + _____ + _____ + _____

6. Write 42,584 in expanded form. _____ + _____ + _____ + _____ + _____

7. Write 40 + 500 + 7 + 8,000 in standard form. _____

8. Write 60 + 900 + 9,000 in standard form. _____

9. Write 18,353 in expanded form. _____ + _____ + _____ + _____ + _____

10. Write 36,444 in expanded form. _____ + _____ + _____ + _____ + _____

Diagnostic Test: Numeration

Directions: Write your answer to each question in the space provided.

Part II: Ordering and Comparing Numbers

1. What number is 1,000 more than 3,287?

   _____

2. What number comes next?

   2,100, 2,200, _____

3. What number is 1,000 less than 6,542?

   _____

4. Write the numbers in order from least to greatest.

   3,200, 2,800, 4,500

   _____ _____ _____

5. Write the numbers in order from least to greatest.

   2,800, 256, 2,785

   _____ _____ _____

6. Use <, >, or = to compare the numbers.

   2,600 2,900

7. Use <, >, or = to compare
    the numbers.

    3,450   (⋯)   3,470

8. Use <, >, or = to compare
    the numbers.

    4,247   (⋯)   4,269

9. Use <, >, or = to compare
    the numbers.

    18,541   (⋯)   17,541

10. Use <, >, or = to compare
    the numbers.

    26,378   (⋯)   26,388

TEACHER ASSESSMENT AREA

Directions: Shade the boxes that correspond to correct test items.

Skill	Item Number				
Ordering Numbers	1	2	3	4	5
Comparing Numbers	6	7	8	9	10

TOTAL CORRECT: _____

Teacher Notes and Activities

TEACHER NOTES: Ordering Numbers
(Diagnostic Test Part II: Test Items 1–5)

Use the concepts of "1,000 more than" and "1,000 less than" to introduce ordering large numbers. A place value chart will help students identify order by comparing digits and place values.

TEACHING ACTIVITIES: "Charting 1,000 Less and More"
(Ordering Numbers)

Using a place value chart, instruct students to chart a number into the thousands period. Then, ask students to chart the number that is 1,000 more or less.

1

2,465

THOUSANDS				ONES		
Hundreds	Tens	Ones		Hundreds	Tens	Ones
		2	,	4	6	5

"What number is 1,000 more?"

THOUSANDS				ONES		
Hundreds	Tens	Ones		Hundreds	Tens	Ones
		3	,	4	6	5

3,465

2

18,342

THOUSANDS				ONES		
Hundreds	Tens	Ones		Hundreds	Tens	Ones
	1	8	,	3	4	2

"What number is 1,000 less?"

THOUSANDS				ONES		
Hundreds	Tens	Ones		Hundreds	Tens	Ones
	1	7	,	3	4	2

17,342

For students who experience difficulty, demonstrate how to model the numbers using base ten blocks. They should physically add or take away a thousand cube, count each place value, and write the new number.

"Order Please" (Ordering Numbers)

Give each student a copy of the ten thousand chart below. Also, show a transparency of the chart on an overhead projector. Ask students to count out loud from 1,000 to 10,000, first by hundreds and then by thousands.

TEN THOUSAND CHART

100	200	300	400	500	600	700	800	900	1,000
1,100	1,200	1,300	1,400	1,500	1,600	1,700	1,800	1,900	2,000
2,100	2,200	2,300	2,400	2,500	2,600	2,700	2,800	2,900	3,000
3,100	3,200	3,300	3,400	3,500	3,600	3,700	3,800	3,900	4,000
4,100	4,200	4,300	4,400	4,500	4,600	4,700	4,800	4,900	5,000
5,100	5,200	5,300	5,400	5,500	5,600	5,700	5,800	5,900	6,000
6,100	6,200	6,300	6,400	6,500	6,600	6,700	6,800	6,900	7,000
7,100	7,200	7,300	7,400	7,500	7,600	7,700	7,800	7,900	8,000
8,100	8,200	8,300	8,400	8,500	8,600	8,700	8,800	8,900	9,000
9,100	9,200	9,300	9,400	9,500	9,600	9,700	9,800	9,900	10,000

Use the ten thousand chart to practice finding 100 more or less and 1,000 more or less.

Point to **5,400**. Ask, "What number is 1,000 more?" Count down one to **6,400**.

Point to **7,700**. Ask, "What number is 100 less?" Count back one to **7,600**.

Continue asking similar questions until students discover a pattern and master 100 more or less and 1,000 more or less. Then, ask students to order sets of numbers using the chart.

Write three numbers on a chalkboard: **4,700, 4,100, 3,900**. Students should use the chart to write the numbers in order from least to greatest: **3,900, 4,100, 4,700**.

"Least to Greatest" (Ordering Numbers)

On index cards or card stock, make a set of 60 number cards. Include a random assortment of numbers between 100 and 10,000. Shuffle the cards. Choose a student to draw four cards and write the card numbers on a chalkboard. Ask the class to order the four numbers in order from least to greatest. Continue the game until all cards have been drawn and the class has ordered all of the numbers.

A student draws the following cards:

1,350	8,590	599	5,675

Instruct the class to order the numbers from least to greatest.

599	1,350	5,675	8,590

Variation: Help students make their own number cards. Then, let students play "Least to Greatest" in groups of four.

TEACHER NOTES: Comparing Numbers (Diagnostic Test Part II: Test Items 6–10)

Students must learn how to order large numbers by comparing digits from the thousands place to the ones place. Begin with easier examples in which the thousands places are the same and the hundreds places are different. Then, move on to more difficult examples in which students must compare digits down to the tens or ones places.

TEACHING ACTIVITY: "Which Number Is Bigger?" (Comparing Numbers)

Demonstrate for students how to compare large numbers by following the steps listed below.

Step 1: Compare the one thousands places. If they are the same, continue to step 2.

Step 2: Compare the hundreds places. If they are the same, continue to step 3.

Step 3: Compare the tens places. If they are the same, continue to step 4.

Step 4: Compare the ones places. If they are the same, the numbers are equal.

NUMERATION PART II: ORDERING AND COMPARING NUMBERS

After reviewing the steps above, ask students to practice comparing pairs of numbers between 1,000 and 9,999. Follow the steps to determine which number is larger. Instruct students to write the number pairs on their sheets of paper and use the <, >, or = sign to compare each pair of numbers.

Comparing thousands:	3,458	2,458	Comparing tens:	6,480	6,450
	7,567	8,467		4,589	4,539
	5,098	4,098		2,750	2,790
Comparing hundreds:	5,325	5,125	Comparing ones:	5,789	5,783
	6,710	6,910		7,945	7,941
	4,383	8,110		4,965	4,969

Demonstrate for students how to use place value charts to help them compare numbers.

Compare 2,347 and 2,389.

THOUSANDS				ONES		
Hundreds	Tens	Ones		Hundreds	Tens	Ones
		2		3	4	7
		2	,	3	8	9

When students have mastered comparing numbers into the thousands place, introduce larger numbers.

CD-104225 • Jump Into Math • © Carson-Dellosa

More or Less

Directions: Write the number that is 10, 100, 1,000, or 10,000 more or less than each number.

1. What number is 10 more than 452?

_____

2. What number is 100 more than 1,273?

_____

3. What number is 1,000 less than 6,420?

_____

4. What number is 10,000 more than 6,420?

_____

5. What number is 100 more than 5,108?

_____

6. What number is 1,000 more than 73,437?

_____

7. What number is 1,000 less than 11,624?

_____

8. What number is 10,000 less than 67,426?

_____

9. What number is 100 less than 3,333?

_____

10. What number is 1,000 less than 40,000?

_____

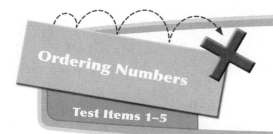

What Comes Next?

Directions: Fill in the missing numbers in the number patterns below.

1. 1,354, _____ , _____ , 1,357, 1,358, _____ , _____ , _____ , 1,362

2. 5,110, 5,120, _____ , _____ , 5,150, _____ , _____ , 5,180, _____

3. 3,100, 3,200, _____ , _____ , _____ , 3,600, _____ , _____ , 3,900

4. 11,722, _____ , 11,742, _____ , _____ , _____ , 11,782, _____

5. 6,000, 7,000, _____ , _____ , 10,000, _____ , _____ , _____

Directions: Write the number that comes before, between, or after.

BEFORE		BETWEEN			AFTER	
6. _____	1,546	13. 3,422 _____	3,424	20. 5,288	_____	
7. _____	3,124	14. 8,129 _____	8,131	21. 2,459	_____	
8. _____	5,555	15. 6,600 _____	6,602	22. 7,679	_____	
9. _____	7,801	16. 4,989 _____	4,991	23. 3,000	_____	
10. _____	4,330	17. 4,599 _____	4,601	24. 1,764	_____	
11. _____	6,700	18. 2,215 _____	2,217	25. 5,599	_____	
12. _____	9,981	19. 9,378 _____	9,380	26. 8,821	_____	

CD-104225 • Jump Into Math • © Carson-Dellosa

Order Please

Ordering Numbers

Test Items 1–5

Directions: Study the ten thousand chart below. Then, answer the following questions.

TEN THOUSAND CHART

100	200	300	400	500	600	700	800	900	1,000
1,100	1,200	1,300	1,400	1,500	1,600	1,700	1,800	1,900	2,000
2,100	2,200	2,300	2,400	2,500	2,600	2,700	2,800	2,900	3,000
3,100	3,200	3,300	3,400	3,500	3,600	3,700	3,800	3,900	4,000
4,100	4,200	4,300	4,400	4,500	4,600	4,700	4,800	4,900	5,000
5,100	5,200	5,300	5,400	5,500	5,600	5,700	5,800	5,900	6,000
6,100	6,200	6,300	6,400	6,500	6,600	6,700	6,800	6,900	7,000
7,100	7,200	7,300	7,400	7,500	7,600	7,700	7,800	7,900	8,000
8,100	8,200	8,300	8,400	8,500	8,600	8,700	8,800	8,900	9,000
9,100	9,200	9,300	9,400	9,500	9,600	9,700	9,800	9,900	10,000

1. What number is 1,000 more than 3,200? _____

2. What number is 1,000 less than 5,500? _____

3. What number is 100 more than 2,700? _____

4. What number is 1,000 more than 6,200? _____

5. What number is 1,000 less than 4,400? _____

6. What number is 100 less than 7,200? _____

7. What number is 1,000 more than 8,200? _____

8. What number is 100 more than 7,900? _____

9. What number is 1,000 more than 9,000? _____

Ordering Numbers

Test Items 1–5

What Comes Next?

Directions: Using the lines below each set of treasure chests, write the numbers in order from least to greatest.

1.

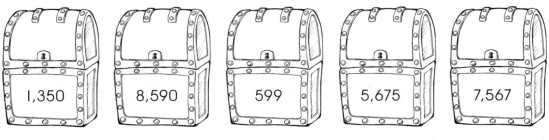

1,350   8,590   599   5,675   7,567

_____ _____ _____ _____ _____

2.

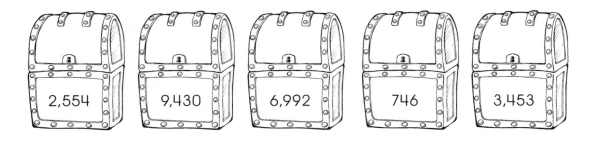

2,554   9,430   6,992   746   3,453

_____ _____ _____ _____ _____

Directions: Using the lines below the set of treasure chests, write the numbers in order from greatest to least.

3.

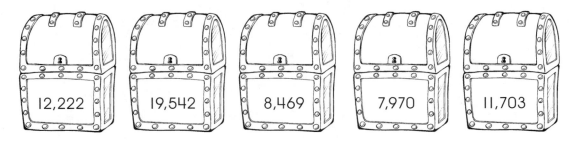

12,222   19,542   8,469   7,970   11,703

_____ _____ _____ _____ _____

Comparing Large Numbers

Comparing Numbers

Test Items 6–10

Directions: Compare the numbers below. Write > (greater than), < (less than), or = (equal to) in each circle.

1. 3,458 ◯ 2,458

2. 4,588 ◯ 4,588

3. 6,710 ◯ 6,910

4. 2,596 ◯ 2,596

5. 1,347 ◯ 1,374

6. 2,790 ◯ 2,750

7. 5,325 ◯ 5,125

8. 9,731 ◯ 9,713

9. 7,945 ◯ 7,941

10. 8,438 ◯ 8,110

11. 8,500 ◯ 8,499

12. 6,792 ◯ 66,792

13. 12,356 ◯ 13,356

14. 19,675 ◯ 19,625

15. 22,370 ◯ 22,377

16. 45,732 ◯ 45,785

17. 56,795 ◯ 56,795

18. 89,280 ◯ 89,180

Diagnostic Test: Addition and Subtraction

Directions: Add and write your answer to each question in the space provided.

Part I: Addition with and without Regrouping

1.
```
   317
 +  46
```

4.
```
   2,345
 + 2,434
```

2.
```
   413
 + 384
```

5.
```
   5,676
 + 7,428
```

3.
```
   4,613
 + 3,479
```

6.
```
   2,000
     200
 +   500
```

NAME: _____   DATE: _____

7.	5,782	9.	4,623
	348		375
	+ 230		+ 413

8.	2,545	10.	387
	173		496
	+ 432		+ 124

TEACHER ASSESSMENT AREA

Directions: Shade the boxes that correspond to correct test items.

Skill	Item Number				
Three- and Four-Digit Addition	1	2	3	4	5
Adding More Than Two Numbers	6	7	8	9	10

TOTAL CORRECT: _____

Teacher Notes and Activities

TEACHER NOTES: Three- and Four-Digit Addition
(Diagnostic Test Part I: Test Items 1–5)

Review the addition algorithm and include four-digit numbers. For struggling learners, begin with physical models such as base ten blocks. Most third-grade students should have mastered place value to the thousands and can utilize the abstract process of "mark out and regroup" presented below. However, students who experience difficulty may need to use place value charts.

TEACHING ACTIVITY: "Step-by-Step Demonstration" (Three- and Four-Digit Addition)

Demonstrate four-digit addition using the steps listed below. Help students work through each step as you complete the problem.

5,712 + 5,389

Step 1: Add the ones.
Regroup if needed.
Think: 2 + 9 = 11 (1 ten, 1 one)

$$\begin{array}{r} 1 \\ 5,71\mathbf{2} \\ + 5,38\mathbf{9} \\ \hline \mathbf{1} \end{array}$$

Step 2: Add the tens.
Regroup if needed.
Think: 10 + 10 + 80 = 100
1 hundred, 0 tens

$$\begin{array}{r} 1\,1 \\ 5,7\mathbf{1}2 \\ + 5,3\mathbf{8}9 \\ \hline \mathbf{0}1 \end{array}$$

Step 3: Add the hundreds.
Regroup if needed.
Think: 100 + 700 + 300 = 1,100
1 thousand, 1 hundred

$$\begin{array}{r} 1\,1\,1 \\ 5,\mathbf{7}12 \\ + 5,\mathbf{3}89 \\ \hline \mathbf{1}01 \end{array}$$

Step 4: Add the thousands.
Regroup to the ten thousands place if needed.
Think: 1,000 + 5,000 + 5,000 = 11,000
1 ten thousand, 1 thousand

$$\begin{array}{r} 1\,1\;\,1\,1 \\ \mathbf{5},712 \\ + \mathbf{5},389 \\ \hline \mathbf{11},101 \end{array}$$

    CD-104225 • Jump Into Math • © Carson-Dellosa

Demonstrate as many problems as needed to help students understand and memorize the addition steps. Display the steps on a prominent place in your classroom, such as a bulletin board or wall poster.

TEACHER NOTES: Adding More than Two Numbers

(Diagnostic Test Part I: Test Items 6–10)

Review the Associative Property of Addition. This property helps students add three numbers by allowing them to add digits in groups of tens or doubles.

ASSOCIATIVE PROPERTY OF ADDITION

The Associative Property of Addition allows addends to be grouped and added in any order without changing the sum. Example: $(7 + 3) + 3 = 13$ and $7 + (3 + 3) = 13$.

TEACHING ACTIVITY: "Addition Strategies" (Adding More than Two Numbers)

Demonstrate the addition of three numbers by following the steps presented on page 32. Talk about each step and help students see how the associative property helps in the addition process.

5,784 + 348 + 242

Step 1: Add the ones.
    Regroup if needed.
    Think: Tens
    $4 + (8 + 2) = 4 + 10 = 14$
    1 ten, 4 ones

$$
\begin{array}{r}
\overset{\textstyle 1}{}\\
5,78\mathbf{4}\\
34\mathbf{8}\\
+\quad 24\mathbf{2}\\
\hline
\mathbf{4}
\end{array}
$$

Step 2: Add the tens.
    Regroup if needed.
    Think: Doubles
    $(4 + 4) + 8 + 1 = (8 + 8) + 1 = 16 + 1 = 17$
    1 hundred, 7 tens

$$
\begin{array}{r}
\overset{\textstyle 1\,1}{}\\
5,7\mathbf{8}4\\
34\mathbf{8}\\
+\quad 2\mathbf{4}2\\
\hline
\mathbf{7}4
\end{array}
$$

Step 3: Add the hundreds.
    Regroup if needed.
    Think: Tens
    $(7 + 3) + 2 + 1 = 10 + 2 + 7 = 12 + 1 = 13$
    1 thousand, 3 hundreds

$$
\begin{array}{r}
\overset{\textstyle 1\;1\,1}{}\\
5,\mathbf{7}84\\
\mathbf{3}48\\
+\quad \mathbf{2}42\\
\hline
\mathbf{3}74
\end{array}
$$

Step 4: Add the thousands.
    Regroup if needed.
    Think: $5 + 1 = 6$
    6 thousands

$$
\begin{array}{r}
\overset{\textstyle 1\;1\,1}{}\\
\mathbf{5},784\\
348\\
+\quad 242\\
\hline
\mathbf{6},374
\end{array}
$$

Allow students to practice as many problems as needed to master the concept. Ask them to verbalize each step as they practice at the chalkboard and demonstrate for the class.

No Need to Regroup

Three- and Four-Digit Addition

Test Items 1–5

Directions: Study the example. Then, solve the following addition problems.

Example:
To find the sum, add the digits in the ones place first. Then, add the digits in the tens place. Finally, add the digits in the hundreds place.

	ones	**tens**	**hundreds**
134	134	134	134
+ 245	+ 245	+ 245	+ 245
	9	79	379

1. 315
    + 44

2. 446
    + 31

3. 173
    + 13

4. 517
    + 51

5. 653
    + 25

6. 881
    + 116

7. 418
    + 250

8. 888
    + 110

9. 581
    + 316

10. 774
    + 223

11. 607
    + 242

12. 732
    + 222

13. 4,725
    + 2,140

14. 8,361
    + 1,026

15. 2,444
    + 5,155

16. 1,638
    + 4,261

Remember Regrouping

Three- and Four-Digit Addition

Test Items 1–5

Directions: Study the example. Then, solve the following addition problems.

Example: To find the sum, add the digits in the ones place first. Regroup if needed. Then, add the digits in the tens place. Regroup if necessary. Next, add the digits in the hundreds place. Regroup if necessary. Finally, add the digits in the thousands place. Regroup to the ten thousands place if necessary.

```
    1              1 1            1  1 1          1 1  1 1
  5,71 2          5,71 2          5,7 1 2          5,7 1 2
+ 5,38 9        + 5,3 8 9        + 5,3 89        + 5,389
------          ------          ------          ------
     1              0 1            1 0 1          1 1,1 0 1
```

1. 2,408
  + 2,675

2. 3,496
  + 2,576

3. 5,322
  + 1,748

4. 8,921
  + 3,779

5. 3,993
  + 5,657

6. 6,089
  + 3,783

7. 7,363
  + 4,567

8. 2,647
  + 4,453

9. 5,154
  + 4,846

10. 9,372
   + 2,578

11. 4,905
   + 2,895

12. 9,302
   + 4,598

13. 7,352
   + 2,783

14. 4,284
   + 5,746

15. 1,801
   + 6,539

16. 3,619
   + 7,525

CD-104225 • Jump Into Math • © Carson-Dellosa

Practice Regrouping

Three- and Four-Digit Addition

Test Items 1–5

Directions: Find the sum for each problem.

1. $\begin{array}{r} 1,104 \\ +\ 2,424 \\ \hline \end{array}$

2. $\begin{array}{r} 9,919 \\ +\ \ \ \ 38 \\ \hline \end{array}$

3. $\begin{array}{r} 20 \\ +\ 657 \\ \hline \end{array}$

4. $\begin{array}{r} 4,489 \\ +\ \ \ \ 11 \\ \hline \end{array}$

5. $\begin{array}{r} 2,760 \\ +\ \ 905 \\ \hline \end{array}$

6. $\begin{array}{r} 2,732 \\ +\ \ 770 \\ \hline \end{array}$

7. $\begin{array}{r} 5,676 \\ +\ 5,936 \\ \hline \end{array}$

8. $\begin{array}{r} 1,979 \\ +\ \ 412 \\ \hline \end{array}$

9. $\begin{array}{r} 763 \\ +\ 255 \\ \hline \end{array}$

10. $\begin{array}{r} 4,597 \\ +\ \ 106 \\ \hline \end{array}$

11. $\begin{array}{r} 7,371 \\ +\ \ 551 \\ \hline \end{array}$

12. $\begin{array}{r} 8,599 \\ +\ \ 299 \\ \hline \end{array}$

13. $\begin{array}{r} 8,121 \\ +\ \ \ 68 \\ \hline \end{array}$

14. $\begin{array}{r} 5,019 \\ +\ \ 252 \\ \hline \end{array}$

15. $\begin{array}{r} 7,314 \\ +\ 1,859 \\ \hline \end{array}$

Three- and Four-Digit Addition

Test Items 1–5

Can You Find the Missing Digits?

Directions: Look at each addition problem. Find the missing digits.

1.
```
    5  □
+   □  7
───────
    8  9
```

2.
```
  4  5  7
+     4  □
─────────
  □  □  8
```

3.
```
     6  7
+  □  2
─────────
  9  □
```

4.
```
     □  □
+    6  9
────────
  □  3  9
```

5.
```
  5  7  3
+     2  □
─────────
  5  □  7
```

6.
```
  □  □  0
+     4  0
─────────
  9  8  □
```

7.
```
  6  □  □
+     4  1
─────────
  □  2  5
```

8.
```
  □  8  7
+  9  9  □
──────────
1,8 □  7
```

9.
```
  4  1  □
+  □  5
─────────
  □  9  9
```

CD-104225 • Jump Into Math • © Carson-Dellosa

More Missing Digits

Three- and Four-Digit Addition

Test Items 1–5

Directions: Look at each addition problem. Find the missing digits.

1.
```
    2  6  7
 +  2  7 □
 ─────────
  □ □   5
```

2.
```
  □ , □ □ □
+ 7 , 7 0 3
───────────
 14 , 3 8 5
```

3.
```
  □ , 7  1  □
 +     4  5  2
─────────────
  9 , □ □  5
```

4.
```
  □ , 6  0  1
+ 8 , □  2  5
─────────────
 10 , 1 □ □
```

5.
```
  □ , 2  4  2
 +    □ □  9
─────────────
  1 , 5  8 □
```

6.
```
  □ , 3  3  5
+ 5 , 6  0  2
─────────────
  9 , □ □ □
```

NAME: _____ DATE: _____

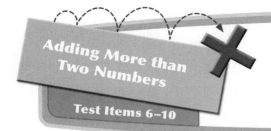

Adding Multiple Numbers

Directions: Solve the following addition problems.

To find the sum, add the digits in the ones place first. Regroup if necessary. Then, add the digits in the tens place. Regroup if necessary. Next, add the digits in the hundreds place. Regroup if necessary. Finally, add the digits in the thousands place. Regroup if necessary.

1.
```
   735
    89
+ 104
```

2.
```
   201
    96
+ 382
```

3.
```
   322
   174
+ 456
```

4.
```
   443
   602
+ 217
```

5.
```
   612
   149
+ 240
```

6.
```
   523
   431
+  77
```

7.
```
   631
   211
+ 431
```

8.
```
   574
   281
+ 342
```

9.
```
   245
   441
+  63
```

10.
```
   385
   195
+  55
```

11.
```
   284
   711
+ 245
```

12.
```
   492
   456
+ 735
```

13.
```
   463
    23
+ 523
```

14.
```
   219
   166
+ 222
```

15.
```
   372
   541
+ 635
```

16.
```
   6,039
   2,680
+ 3,435
```

17.
```
   2,801
   1,426
+ 4,391
```

18.
```
   8,230
   1,546
+   666
```

19.
```
   7,621
   6,587
+ 1,423
```

20.
```
   5,556
   2,162
+ 3,324
```

CD-104225 • Jump Into Math • © Carson-Dellosa

Adding It Up

Adding More than Two Numbers

Test Items 6–10

Directions: Solve the following addition problems.

I.	1,104 2,424 + 618		2.	9,919 128 + 354		3.	4,489 1,367 + 480

4.	2,573 476 + 12		5.	2,760 3,240 + 10		6.	5.760 2,905 + 98

7.	763 2,402 + 1,005		8.	678 235 + 3,400		9.	510 233 + 578

10.	4,502 1,007 + 25		II.	2,004 1,308 + 102		12.	3,508 1,235 + 1,301

13.	1,590 2,214 + 306		14.	3,450 1,278 + 1,103		15.	5,102 1,033 + 1,277

Diagnostic Test: Addition and Subtraction

Directions: Subtract and write your answer to each question in the space provided.

Part II: Subtraction with and without Regrouping

1. $8 - 5$ = _____

  $80 - 50$ = _____

  $800 - 500$ = _____

4.   307
  − 29
  ———

2. $20 - 10$ = _____

  $200 - 100$ = _____

  $2,000 - 1,000$ = _____

5.   400
  − 215
  ———

6.   589
  − 375
  ———

3.   203
  − 125
  ———

7.   676
      − 354

9.   7,457
      − 4,286

8.   5,324
      − 1,367

10.   6,457
      − 3,659

TEACHER ASSESSMENT AREA

Directions: Shade the boxes that correspond to correct test items.

TOTAL CORRECT: _____

Skill	Item Number				
Subtraction Patterns	1	2			
Subtraction across Zeros	3	4	5		
Three- and Four-Digit Subtraction	6	7	8	9	10

Teacher Notes and Activities

TEACHER NOTES: Subtraction Patterns
(Diagnostic Test Part II: Test Items 1–2)

Use students' knowledge of place value and basic subtraction facts to prepare them for subtraction of three- and four-digit numbers. Subtraction patterns will help students see the relationship between basic facts and multiples of 10, 100, and 1,000. The development of this math strategy will strengthen the development of the subtraction algorithm.

TEACHING ACTIVITIES

"Pattern Posters" (Subtraction Patterns)

Review basic subtraction facts and counting by multiples of 10, 100, and 1,000. Help students to discover the pattern. Make a poster for the following subtraction facts and multiples of those facts. Ask students to study the poster and find the pattern.

Guess My Pattern

$7 - 4 =$ _____ $8 - 3 =$ _____

$70 - 40 =$ _____ $80 - 30 =$ _____

$700 - 400 =$ _____ $800 - 300 =$ _____

     $8,000 - 3,000 =$ _____

$9 - 5 =$ _____ $80,000 - 30,000 =$ _____

$90 - 50 =$ _____

$900 - 500 =$ _____ $6 - 2 =$ _____

     $60 - 20 =$ _____

$5 - 1 =$ _____ $600 - 200 =$ _____

$50 - 10 =$ _____ $6,000 - 2,000 =$ _____

$500 - 100 =$ _____ $60,000 - 20,000 =$ _____

"Mental Math" (Subtraction Patterns)

Play this game with students. Say, "Can you guess what I'm thinking? Write my thoughts as subtraction facts."

You say:	Students write:
10 ones – 5 ones =	$10 - 5 = 5$
10 tens – 5 tens =	$100 - 50 = 50$
10 hundreds – 5 hundreds =	$1,000 - 500 = 500$

You say: **Students write:**

9 ones – 5 ones =   _____ – _____ = _____

9 tens – 5 tens =   _____ – _____ = _____

9 hundreds – 5 hundreds =   _____ – _____ = _____

9 thousands – 5 thousands =   _____ – _____ = _____

TEACHER NOTES: Subtracting across Zeros

(Diagnostic Test Part II: Test Items 3–5)

One of the most troublesome aspects of subtraction is regrouping across zeros. It is a very common source of student errors. To overcome this, developmental work must be completed and practiced by students. You should provide developmental instruction and activities such as shown below before moving students on to the subtraction algorithm.

TEACHING ACTIVITY: "1 Less Hundred, 10 More Tens" (Subtracting across Zeros)

Instruct students to regroup each number so that there is 1 less hundred and 10 more tens, then 1 less ten and 10 more ones. The first number has been completed as an example.

NUMBER	1 LESS HUNDRED 10 MORE TENS	1 LESS TEN 10 MORE ONES
300	2 10 $\cancel{3}\,\cancel{0}\,0$	9 2 $\cancel{0}$ 10 $\cancel{3}\,\cancel{0}\,\cancel{0}$
600		
304		
207		
501		

TEACHER NOTES: Three- and Four-Digit Subtraction
(Diagnostic Test Part II: Test Items 6–10)

Errors are also common in subtraction problems that require regrouping two or three times. Use developmental activities to reinforce the concept of regrouping before attempting the subtraction algorithm.

TEACHING ACTIVITIES: "Regrouping Tens and Ones"

(Three- and Four-Digit Subtraction)

Ask students to regroup each number by showing 1 less ten and 10 more ones.

83 → __7/8__ tens   __13/3__ ones

61 → _____ tens   _____ ones

96 → _____ tens   _____ ones

49 → _____ tens   _____ ones

"Regrouping Hundreds and Tens" (Three- and Four-Digit Subtraction)

Ask students to regroup each number by showing 1 less hundred and 10 more tens.

246 → __1/2__ hundreds   __14/4__ tens   __6__ ones

705 → _____ hundreds   _____ tens   _____ ones

563 → _____ hundreds   _____ tens   _____ ones

999 → _____ hundreds   _____ tens   _____ ones

"Subtracting Three-Digit Numbers" (Three- and Four-Digit Subtraction)

Lead students through the steps below to subtract three-digit numbers.

563 – 278

Step 1: Compare the ones.
Regroup the tens.
Subtract the ones.

$$\begin{array}{r} 5\ \mathbf{13} \\ 5\ \cancel{6}\ \mathbf{3} \\ -\ 2\ 7\ \mathbf{8} \\ \hline \mathbf{5} \end{array}$$

Step 2: Compare the tens.
Regroup the hundreds.
Subtract the tens.

$$\begin{array}{r} \mathbf{15} \\ 4\ \cancel{5}\ 13 \\ \cancel{5}\ \mathbf{6}\ \cancel{3} \\ -\ 2\ \mathbf{7}\ 8 \\ \hline \mathbf{8}\ 5 \end{array}$$

Step 3: Compare the hundreds.
Subtract the hundreds.

$$\begin{array}{r} 15 \\ 4\ \cancel{5}\ 13 \\ \cancel{5}\ \cancel{6}\ \cancel{3} \\ -\ \mathbf{2}\ 7\ 8 \\ \hline \mathbf{2}\ 8\ 5 \end{array}$$

Allow students to practice with several similar problems. Instruct them to follow each step and discuss their work after each step. It is important that students can verbally explain each step as they complete it.

"Subtracting Four-Digit Numbers" (Three- and Four-Digit Subtraction)

Follow the steps below to subtract four-digit numbers. Instruct students to study the example carefully.

2,238 – 1,319

Step 1: Compare the ones.
Regroup the tens.
Subtract the ones.

$$\begin{array}{r} {\scriptstyle 2\ 18} \\ 2,2\cancel{3}\cancel{8} \\ -\ 1,3\ 1\ 9 \\ \hline 9 \end{array}$$

Step 2: Compare the tens.
Regroup the hundreds.
Subtract the tens.

$$\begin{array}{r} {\scriptstyle \mathbf{2}\ 18} \\ 2,2\cancel{3}\cancel{8} \\ -\ 1,3\ 1\ 9 \\ \hline 1\ 9 \end{array}$$

Step 3: Compare the hundreds.
Regroup the thousands.
Subtract the hundreds.

$$\begin{array}{r} {\scriptstyle 1\ \ \mathbf{12}\ \ 2\ 18} \\ \cancel{2},\cancel{2}\cancel{3}\cancel{8} \\ -\ 1,3\ 1\ 9 \\ \hline \mathbf{9}\ 1\ 9 \end{array}$$

Step 4: Compare the thousands.
Subtract the thousands.

$$\begin{array}{r} {\scriptstyle 1\ \ 12\ \ 2\ 18} \\ \mathbf{\cancel{2}},\cancel{2}\cancel{3}\cancel{8} \\ -\ \mathbf{1},3\ 1\ 9 \\ \hline 1,9\ 1\ 9 \end{array}$$

Allow students to practice with several similar problems. Instruct them to follow each step and discuss their work after each step. It is important that students can verbally explain each step as they complete it.

Find My Pattern

Subtraction Patterns

Test Items 1–2

Directions: Subtract to find the pattern in each of the following problems. Write your answers in the spaces provided.

1.   6 – 4   = _____
    60 – 40   = _____
    600 – 400   = _____

2.   8 – 5   = _____
    80 – 50   = _____
    800 – 500   = _____

3.   7 – 4   = _____
    70 – 40   = _____
    700 – 400   = _____

4.   9 – 5   = _____
    90 – 50   = _____
    900 – 500   = _____
    9,000 – 5,000   = _____

5.   5 – 3   = _____
    50 – 30   = _____
    500 – 300   = _____
    5,000 – 3,000   = _____
    50,000 – 30,000   = _____

6.   10 – 5   = _____
    100 – 50   = _____
    1,000 – 500   = _____

7.   20 – 10   = _____
    200 – 100   = _____
    2,000 – 1,000   = _____

8.   6 – 2   = _____
    60 – 20   = _____
    600 – 200   = _____

9.   5 ones – 3 ones   = _____
    5 tens – 3 tens   = _____
    5 hundreds – 3 hundreds   = _____
    5 thousands – 3 thousands   = _____

10.   9 ones – 4 ones   = _____
    9 tens – 4 tens   = _____
    9 hundreds – 4 hundreds   = _____
    9 thousands – 4 thousands   = _____

Regrouping Zeros

Directions: Regroup each number so that there is 1 less hundred and 10 more tens, then 1 less ten and 10 more ones. The first problem has been completed for you.

NUMBER	1 LESS HUNDRED 10 MORE TENS	1 LESS TEN 10 MORE ONES
1. 300	2 10 3̸ 0̸ 0	9 2 0̸ 10 3̸ 0̸ 0̸
2. 600		
3. 304		
4. 207		
5. 501		
6. 403		
7. 706		
8. 910		
9. 800		
10. 606		

CD-104225 • Jump Into Math • © Carson-Dellosa

Lots of Zeros

Subtraction across Zeros

Test Items 3–5

Directions: Solve each subtraction problem. Regroup when needed.

Example:

```
    6 9 10
    7 Ø Ø
  - 5 4 5
    1 5 5
```

1.
```
    400
  - 128
```

2.
```
    500
  - 345
```

3.
```
    700
  - 569
```

4.
```
    800
  - 751
```

5.
```
    900
  - 555
```

6.
```
    370
  - 254
```

7.
```
    608
  - 553
```

8.
```
    904
  - 735
```

9.
```
    200
  -  89
```

Regrouping

Directions: Study the example carefully. Then, subtract the following problems. Regroup when needed.

Compare the ones first. If the bottom ones digit is greater than the top ones digit, you need to regroup from the tens. Then, compare the tens. If the bottom tens digit is greater than the top tens digit, regroup from the hundreds.

Example:	**Step 1**	**Step 2**	**Step 3**
563 − 278	5 13 5 6 3 − 2 7 8 5	15 4 5 13 5 6 3 − 2 7 8 8 5	15 4 5 13 5 6 3 − 2 7 8 2 8 5

1.　　186
　　− 99

2.　　174
　　− 86

3.　　356
　　− 258

4.　　574
　　− 382

5.　　227
　　− 119

6.　　716
　　− 207

7.　　688
　　− 398

8.　　492
　　− 363

9.　　537
　　− 229

10.　　838
　　− 372

11.　　682
　　− 580

12.　　981
　　− 704

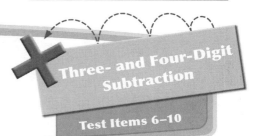

Subtracting Large Numbers

Directions: Subtract the following problems. Regroup when needed.

> **Example:**
> **Step 1:** Subtract the ones. Regroup if needed.
> **Step 2:** Subtract the tens. Regroup if needed.
> **Step 3:** Subtract the hundreds. Regroup if needed.
> **Step 4:** Subtract the thousands.
>
> $$2,238 - 1,319$$
>
> | Step 1 | Step 2 | Step 3 | Step 4 |
> |--------|--------|--------|--------|
> | 2 18
2,23 8
− 1,3 1 9
9 | 2 18
2,2 3 8
− 1,3 1 9
1 9 | 1 12 2 18
2,2 3 8
− 1,3 1 9
9 1 9 | 1 12 2 18
2,2 3 8
− 1,3 1 9
9 1 9 |

1.   2,772
   − 1,376

2.   3,943
   − 1,875

3.   5,915
   − 2,767

4.   9,275
   − 4,879

5.   7,680
   − 3,745

6.   9,700
   − 2,778

7.   5,549
   − 2,460

8.   3,905
   − 1,856

9.   7,976
   − 3,698

10.   8,409
   − 4,628

11.   4,905
   − 2,895

12.   9,302
   − 4,598

Subtracting More Large Numbers

Directions: Subtract. Regroup when needed.

1. 4,534
   − 4,499

2. 6,430
   − 1,704

3. 8,875
   − 6,435

4. 5,311
   − 2,721

5. 6,632
   − 4,454

6. 9,079
   − 3,438

7. 8,921
   − 4,927

8. 9,305
   − 6,814

9. 9,399
   − 7,061

10. 9,416
    − 1,661

11. 8,452
    − 4,978

12. 8,168
    − 4,588

13. 7,352
    − 2,783

14. 8,284
    − 5,746

15. 9,801
    − 6,539

Can You Find the Missing Digits?

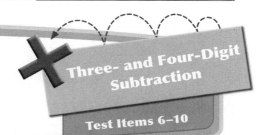

Three- and Four-Digit Subtraction

Test Items 6–10

Directions: Look at each subtraction problem. Write the missing digits.

1.
```
    5 , 9 8 □
  − 5 , □ 6 2
  ───────────
    5   □ 3
```

2.
```
    □ , 9 2 7
  − 2 , □ 1 □
  ───────────
    4 , 7 □ 2
```

3.
```
    9 , 8 □ □
  − □ , 0 8 2
  ───────────
    3 , □ 2 3
```

4.
```
    9 , 6 □ 2
  − □ , 1 7 9
  ───────────
    8 , □ 4 □
```

5.
```
    6 , 2 □ □
  − 4 , 7 2 3
  ───────────
    □ , □ 0 0
```

6.
```
    8 , 4 □ 9
  − □ , □ 2 9
  ───────────
        3 2 □
```

7.
```
    5 , 0 □ 9
  − 3 , □ 0 □
  ───────────
    □ , 4 6 0
```

8.
```
    □ , 5 7 7
  − 1 , 4 7 □
  ───────────
    2 , □ □ 1
```

Diagnostic Test:
Multiplication and Division

Directions: Read each question. Write your answer in the space provided.

Part I: Beginning Multiplication Concepts

1. Write the missing numbers.

    _____ , 12, 14, _____ , 18

2. Write the missing numbers.

    20, 24, _____ , 32, _____

3. Add.

    3 + 3 + 3 + 3 + 3 = _____

4. Add.

    4 + 4 + 4 + 4 = _____

5. Add.

    2 + 2 + 2 + 2 + 2 = _____

6. Add.

    5 + 5 + 5 + 5 + 5 + 5 = _____

7.

    2 rows x 5 in each row = _____

8.

2 rows x 6 in each row = _____

9.

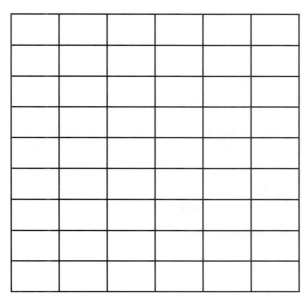

_____ rows x _____ in each row

= _____

10.

_____ rows x _____ in each row

= _____

TEACHER ASSESSMENT AREA

Directions: Shade the boxes that correspond to correct test items.

Skill	Item Number			
Skip Counting	1	2		
Repeated Addition	3	4	5	6
Arrays	7	8	9	10

TOTAL CORRECT: _____

Teacher Notes and Activities

Background Information

Many teachers and textbooks do not devote enough time to concrete, physical representations of multiplication. Early work with multiplication should include the use of models, number lines, arrays, and repeated addition to provide a foundation for multiplication.

Many students have difficulty understanding and memorizing multiplication facts. Much of this difficulty is related to the lack of developmental work preceding fact memorization. Students are often left with few ways to think constructively about multiplication.

TEACHER NOTES: Skip Counting
(Diagnostic Test Part I Test Items 1–2)

Many textbooks and instructional materials provide only limited mention of skip counting. This lack of emphasis on basic multiplication concepts such as skip counting can make multiplication unnecessarily difficult for students. Plan activities that provide practice in skip counting orally. Use rhythmic counting, songs, and audio recording activities that emphasize counting by 2s, 3s, 4s, and 5s.

TEACHING ACTIVITIES: "Counting Sets" (Skip Counting)

Provide opportunities for students to group objects by skip counting. Give students counters or worksheets of groups of objects with 6 to 20 in each group. Help them to group the objects and skip count by 2s, 3s, 4s, and 5s.

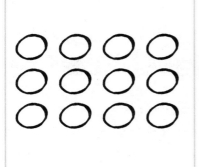

Count by 1s

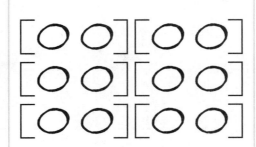

Count by 2s

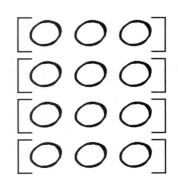

Count by 3s

"Counting Arrays" (Skip Counting)

Give students base ten blocks or other manipulatives. Ask them to form rows and columns by 2s, 3s, 4s, and 5s, then to skip count their blocks.

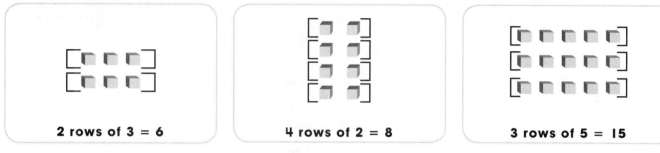

2 rows of 3 = 6   4 rows of 2 = 8   3 rows of 5 = 15

"Number Lines" (Skip Counting)

Encourage students to use number lines to practice skip counting. Give students worksheets with number lines numbered from 1 to 25. Ask students to practice skip counting by 2s, 3s, 4s, and 5s.

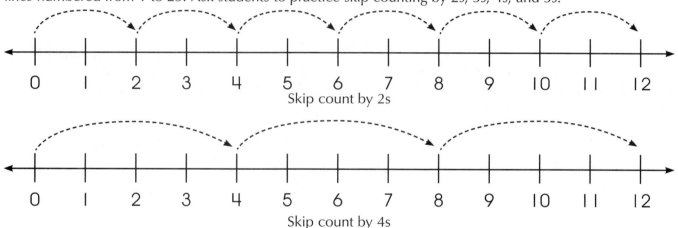

Use a hundred chart to help students practice counting multiples of 2, 3, 4, and 5.

1	2	3	4	5	6	7	8	9	10
11	12	13	14	15	16	17	18	19	20
21	22	23	24	25	26	27	28	29	30
31	32	33	34	35	36	37	38	39	40
41	42	43	44	45	46	47	48	49	50
51	52	53	54	55	56	57	58	59	60
61	62	63	64	65	66	67	68	69	70
71	72	73	74	75	76	77	78	79	80
81	82	83	84	85	86	87	88	89	90
91	92	93	94	95	96	97	98	99	100

TEACHER NOTES: Repeated Addition

(Diagnostic Test Part I: Test Items 3–6)

Repeated addition is a natural extension of students' previous experiences with addition. Repeated addition problems present a given number of sets, each with the same number of objects. The goal is to find the total number of objects. Repeated addition problems can be represented with objects, pictures of objects, or number sentences.

TEACHING ACTIVITY: "Drawing Problems" (Repeated Addition)

Use the following problem as an example. Then, ask students to practice the problems below on their own.

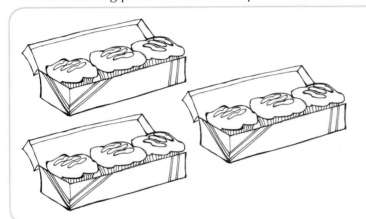

4 packages of cupcakes;

3 cupcakes in each package.

How many cupcakes are there in all?

Number Sentences: $3 + 3 + 3 + 3 = 12$
$4 \times 3 = 12$

Give students the following problems. Ask them to draw a simple picture of each problem, then write the corresponding addition and multiplication problems.

1. 3 baskets of apples;
   2 apples in each basket.
   How many apples in all?

2. 5 shelves of books;
   2 books on each shelf.
   How many books in all?

3. 5 boxes of pencils;
   4 pencils in each box.
   How many pencils in all?

4. 3 groups of cars;
   5 cars in each group.
   How many cars in all?

5. 4 nets with butterflies;
   3 butterflies in each net.
   How many butterflies in all?

6. 4 packages of crayons;
   10 crayons in each package.
   How many crayons in all?

TEACHER NOTES: Arrays

(Diagnostic Test Part I: Test Items 7–10)

Another type of multiplication strategy is the row-by-column representation, or the array. Arrays present a given number of rows, each with the same number of objects. Again, the goal is to find the total number of objects. Arrays can be represented with objects, pictures of objects, or rectangular models made from graph paper.

TEACHING ACTIVITY: "Arrays in Many Ways" (Arrays)

Write the following example on the board:

4 rows of desks; 3 desk in each row. How many in all?

Pictorial representation:

Rectangular model:

Number sentence: 4 rows x 3 in each row = 12 in all

Draw the following on the chalkboard.

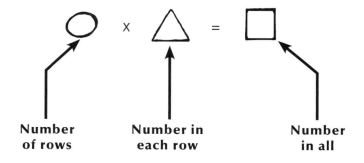

Write a different single-digit number in the circle and in the triangle. Ask students to find how many in all. Show students how to draw arrays to help them answer the question. Then, ask students to give you two numbers between 1 and 5. Write them in the diagram. Ask the class to find out how many in all. Write the multiplication fact for each pair of numbers.

Skip Counting

Directions: Use the hundred chart to skip count by 2s, 3s, 4s, 5s, and 10s.

HUNDRED CHART

1	2	3	4	5	6	7	8	9	10
11	12	13	14	15	16	17	18	19	20
21	22	23	24	25	26	27	28	29	30
31	32	33	34	35	36	37	38	39	40
41	42	43	44	45	46	47	48	49	50
51	52	53	54	55	56	57	58	59	60
61	62	63	64	65	66	67	68	69	70
71	72	73	74	75	76	77	78	79	80
81	82	83	84	85	86	87	88	89	90
91	92	93	94	95	96	97	98	99	100

1. Start at 18 and count by 3s.   18 , ____ , ____ , ____ , ____ , ____

2. Start at 84 and count by 2s.   ____ , ____ , ____ , ____ , ____ , ____

3. Start at 44 and count by 4s.   ____ , ____ , ____ , ____ , ____ , ____

4. Start at 20 and count by 4s.   ____ , ____ , ____ , ____ , ____ , ____

5. Start at 30 and count by 10s.   ____ , ____ , ____ , ____ , ____ , ____

6. Start at 65 and count by 5s.   ____ , ____ , ____ , ____ , ____ , ____

7. Start at 36 and count by 3s.   ____ , ____ , ____ , ____ , ____ , ____

8. Start at 12 and count by 2s.   ____ , ____ , ____ , ____ , ____ , ____

9. Start at 10 and count by 10s.   ____ , ____ , ____ , ____ , ____ , ____

10. Start at 35 and count by 5s.   ____ , ____ , ____ , ____ , ____ , ____

Counting by Groups

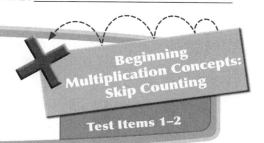

Directions: Look at each group of objects. Skip count to find how many in all.

1. ⎡○○○⎤ ⎡○○○⎤   Count by 3s:
   ⎣○○○⎦ ⎣○○○⎦   ____ , ____ , ____ , ____

2. ⎡◇◇◇◇⎤⎡◇◇◇◇⎤   Count by 4s:
   ⎣◇◇◇◇⎦⎣◇◇◇◇⎦   ____ , ____ , ____ , ____

3. ⎡♡♡⎤ ⎡♡♡⎤
   ⎡♡♡⎤ ⎡♡♡⎤   Count by 2s :
   ⎡♡♡⎤ ⎡♡♡⎤   ____ , ____ , ____ , ____ , ____ , ____ , ____ , ____
   ⎣♡♡⎦ ⎣♡♡⎦

4. ⎡((((((⎤⎡((((((⎤   Count by 5s:
   ⎣((((((⎦⎣((((((⎦   ____ , ____ , ____ , ____

5. ⎡△△△△△△△△△△⎤   Count by 10s :
   ⎢△△△△△△△△△△⎥
   ⎢△△△△△△△△△△⎥   ____ , ____ , ____ , ____
   ⎣△△△△△△△△△△⎦

Find the Multiples

Directions: Study the example. Then, shade the multiples in each chart below.

> 0 is a multiple of all numbers. When you skip count, each number is a multiple of the first number after 0.
> **Example:** Count by 2s. {0, 2, 4, 6, 8, 10, 12, . . .} are multiples of 2.

1. Start with 0. Shade the multiples of 5.

0	1	2	3	4	5	6	7	8
9	10	11	12	13	14	15	16	17
18	19	20	21	22	23	24	25	26
27	28	29	30	31	32	33	34	35
36	37	38	39	40	41	42	43	44

2. Start with 0. Shade the multiples of 2.

0	1	2	3	4	5	6	7	8
9	10	11	12	13	14	15	16	17
18	19	20	21	22	23	24	25	26
27	28	29	30	31	32	33	34	35
36	37	38	39	40	41	42	43	44

3. Start with 0. Shade the multiples of 3.

0	1	2	3	4	5	6	7	8
9	10	11	12	13	14	15	16	17
18	19	20	21	22	23	24	25	26
27	28	29	30	31	32	33	34	35
36	37	38	39	40	41	42	43	44

4. Start with 0. Shade the multiples of 4.

0	1	2	3	4	5	6	7	8
9	10	11	12	13	14	15	16	17
18	19	20	21	22	23	24	25	26
27	28	29	30	31	32	33	34	35
36	37	38	39	40	41	42	43	44

5. Start with 0. Shade the multiples of 6.

0	1	2	3	4	5	6	7	8
9	10	11	12	13	14	15	16	17
18	19	20	21	22	23	24	25	26
27	28	29	30	31	32	33	34	35
36	37	38	39	40	41	42	43	44

6. Start with 0. Shade the multiples of 10.

0	1	2	3	4	5	6	7	8
9	10	11	12	13	14	15	16	17
18	19	20	21	22	23	24	25	26
27	28	29	30	31	32	33	34	35
36	37	38	39	40	41	42	43	44

7. Start with 0. Shade the multiples of 8.

0	1	2	3	4	5	6	7	8
9	10	11	12	13	14	15	16	17
18	19	20	21	22	23	24	25	26
27	28	29	30	31	32	33	34	35
36	37	38	39	40	41	42	43	44

8. Start with 0. Shade the multiples of 7.

0	1	2	3	4	5	6	7	8
9	10	11	12	13	14	15	16	17
18	19	20	21	22	23	24	25	26
27	28	29	30	31	32	33	34	35
36	37	38	39	40	41	42	43	44

CD-104225 • Jump Into Math • © Carson-Dellosa

Multiplying by 2, 5, and 10

Beginning Multiplication Concepts: Skip Counting

Test Items 1–2

Directions: Use skip counting to complete the multiplication table below.

x	0	1	2	3	4	5	6	7	8	9	10
2	0	2	4	6							
5	0	5	10	15							
10	0	10	20	30							

1. 2 x 4 = _____

2. 10 x 1 = _____

3. 5 x 0 = _____

4. 10 x 8 = _____

5. 5 x 3 = _____

6. 2 x 6 = _____

7. 10 x 4 = _____

8. 5 x 2 = _____

9. 2 x 5 = _____

10. 10 x 2 = _____

11. 2 x 9 = _____

12. 5 x 8 = _____

13. 10 x 6 = _____

14. 5 x 5 = _____

15. 2 x 7 = _____

16. 10 x 3 = _____

17. 2 x 8 = _____

18. 5 x 7 = _____

19. 10 x 10 = _____

20. 10 x 9 = _____

Add, Add, Add!

Directions: Draw a line to connect each repeated addition sentence with the matching multiplication sentence.

1. 10 + 10 +10 + 10 = 40

2. 6 + 6 + 6 + 6 = 24

3. 5 + 5 + 5 + 5 + 5 = 25

4. 2 + 2 + 2 + 2 + 2 = 10

5. 2 + 2 + 2 + 2 + 2 + 2 = 12

6. 7 + 7 + 7 = 21

7. 3 + 3 + 3 + 3 + 3 = 15

8. 6 + 6 = 12

9. 4 + 4 + 4 + 4 + 4 = 20

10. 4 + 4 + 4 + 4 = 16

11. 5 + 5 + 5 + 5 + 5 + 5 = 30

12. 3 + 3 + 3 = 9

A. 5 x 5 = 25

B. 4 x 5 = 20

C. 3 x 7 = 21

D. 3 x 3 = 9

E. 2 x 6 = 12

F. 4 x 4 = 16

G. 4 x 6 = 24

H. 5 x 2 = 10

I. 6 x 2 = 12

J. 5 x 3 = 15

K. 4 x 10 = 40

L. 6 x 5 = 30

Adding Groups

Directions: Write an addition sentence and a multiplication sentence for each problem.

1. 3 boxes of pencils;
   4 pencils in each box.
   How many pencils in all?

   ____ + ____ + ____ = ____

   ____ x ____ = ____

2. 4 packages of candy;
   2 candies in each package.
   How many candies in all?

   ____ + ____ + ____ + ____ = ____

   ____ x ____ = ____

3. 4 packs of crayons;
   10 crayons in each pack.
   How many crayons in all?

   ____ + ____ + ____ + ____ = ____

   ____ x ____ = ____

4. 6 bags of marbles;
   5 marbles in each bag.
   How many marbles in all?

   ____ + ____ + ____ + ____ +

   ____ + ____ = ____

   ____ x ____ = ____

5. 5 packs of cupcakes;
   2 cupcakes in each pack.
   How many cupcakes in all?

   ____ + ____ + ____ + ____ + ____ = ____

   ____ x ____ = ____

6. 4 groups of toys;
   6 toys in each group.
   How many toys in all?

   ____ + ____ + ____ + ____ = ____

   ____ x ____ = ____

Beginning
Multiplication Concepts:
Repeated Addition

Test Items 3–6

Group by Group

Directions: Write an addition sentence for each picture.

1.

____ + ____ + ____ = ____

2.

____ + ____ + ____ + ____ = ____

3.

____ + ____ + ____ = ____

4.

____ + ____ = ____

5.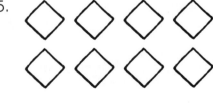

____ + ____ = ____

6.

____ + ____ + ____ = ____

Rows and Columns

Directions: Look at each array. Write a multiplication sentence that describes each array.

Example:

An array is an orderly arrangement of objects in rows and columns.
An egg carton is an example of a 2-by-6 array.

2 rows x 6 in each row = 12
2 x 6 = 12

1.

_____ rows x _____ in each row = _____

_____ x _____ = _____

2.

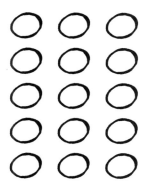

_____ rows x _____ in each row = _____

_____ x _____ = _____

3.

_____ rows x _____ in each row = _____

_____ x _____ = _____

4.

_____ rows x _____ in each row = _____

_____ x _____ = _____

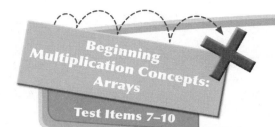

Matching Rows and Columns

Directions: Match each array to the correct multiplication fact at the bottom of the page. Write the correct letter in the blank below each array.

1. [○○○○○○]
   [○○○○○○]
   [○○○○○○]
   [○○○○○○]

   _____

2. [◇◇◇◇◇◇]
   [◇◇◇◇◇◇]

   _____

3. [(((((((((((((]
   [(((((((((((((]
   [(((((((((((((]
   [(((((((((((((]
   [(((((((((((((]

   _____

4. [△△△△△△△△]
   [△△△△△△△△]
   [△△△△△△△△]

   _____

5. [♡♡♡♡]
   [♡♡♡♡]
   [♡♡♡♡]
   [♡♡♡♡]

   _____

6. [☆☆☆☆☆☆☆☆]
   [☆☆☆☆☆☆☆☆]
   [☆☆☆☆☆☆☆☆]
   [☆☆☆☆☆☆☆☆]

   _____

7. [△△△△△△△]

   _____

8. [○○○○○]

   _____

A. 3 x 8

B. 4 x 4

C. 4 x 6

D. 5 x 10

E. 4 x 8

F. 2 x 6

G. 1 x 7

H. 1 x 5

Factors and Products

Beginning Multiplication Concepts: Arrays

Test Items 7–10

Directions: Study the example. Write the number sentence for each problem. Then, find each product.

Example:

You can multiply across.

2 x 3 = 6

You can multiply down.

$$3$$
$$\underline{\times\ 2}$$
$$6$$

1.

_____ X _____ = _____

X

2.

_____ X _____ = _____

X

3.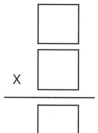

_____ X _____ = _____

X

4.

_____ X _____ = _____

X

Diagnostic Test:
Multiplication and Division

Directions: Read each question. Write your answer in the space provided.

Part II: Beginning Division Concepts

1. There are 15 balls in all. How many equal groups can you make by subtracting groups of 5? Count as you cross them out in the picture.

15 balls ÷ groups of 5 = _____

2. There are 10 fish in all. How many equal groups can you make by subtracting groups of 2? Count as you cross them out in the picture.

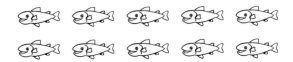

10 fish ÷ groups of 2 = _____

3. There are 12 cupcakes in all. How many equal groups can you make by subtracting groups of 6?

12 cupcakes ÷ groups of 6 = _____

4. There are 8 butterflies in all. How many equal groups can you make by subtracting groups of 2?

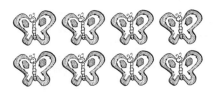

8 butterflies ÷ groups of 2 = _____

5. There are 6 pencils in all. How many equal groups can you make by subtracting groups of 2?

6 pencils ÷ groups of 2 = _____

6. 4 balls; 2 equal groups
   How many in each group?

   $4 \div 2 =$ _____

7. 8 bears; 2 equal groups
   How many in each group?

   $8 \div 2 =$ _____

8. 10 pencils; 2 equal groups
   How many in each group?

   $10 \div 2 =$ _____

9. 12 ducks; 3 equal groups
   How many in each group?

   $12 \div 3 =$ _____

10. 10 butterflies; 5 equal groups
    How many in each group?

    $10 \div 5 =$ _____

TEACHER ASSESSMENT AREA

Directions: Shade the boxes that correspond to correct test items.

Skill	Item Number				
Repeated Subtraction	1	2	3	4	5
Equal Groups	6	7	8	9	10

TOTAL CORRECT: _____

Teacher Notes and Activities

Background Information

Division is one of the most difficult whole-number operations for students to master, as well as one of the most difficult for teachers to teach. To master division, students must be able to correctly use multiplication, subtraction, and addition. The relationship between subtraction and division as well as multiplication and division must be fully understood if students are to divide correctly. Division skills are developed over several grade levels, and care must be exercised to ensure that consistent strategies are used.

TEACHER NOTES: Repeated Subtraction

(Diagnostic Test Part II: Test Items 1–5)

There is a tendency for many teachers to rush into formal division work before students develop a thorough understanding of prerequisite concepts and skills. Be sure that students practice extensively with manipulatives to develop the relationship between repeated subtraction and division, as well as multiplication and division.

TEACHING ACTIVITIES

Demonstrate for students that you can use repeated subtraction to find equal groups. Show 12 objects. Explain that you want to separate the 12 objects into equal groups of 4. You can subtract groups of 4 until you find the number of equal groups.

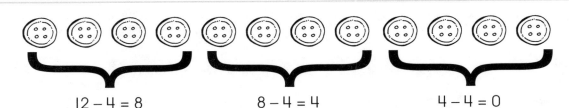

$$12 - 4 = 8 \qquad 8 - 4 = 4 \qquad 4 - 4 = 0$$

There are 3 groups of 4 in 12.

12 divided into groups of 4 equals 3.

$$12 \div 4 = 3$$

"Subtract, Subtract, Subtract" (Repeated Subtraction)

Provide students with the following problems. Use base ten blocks or other manipulatives to represent the total number of objects in each problem. Ask students to determine how many times they must subtract to make the equal groups each problem specifies.

1. There are 10 ducks running loose! Each cage holds 5 ducks. How many cages do you need to hold all 10 ducks?

Use repeated subtraction to find the answer.

How many times did you subtract? _____ times

How many cages do you need? _____ cages

Write the division sentence: 10 ÷ _____ = 5

2. There are 20 cars to load onto trucks. Each truck holds 5 cars. How many trucks do you need?

Use repeated subtraction to find the answer.

How many times did you subtract? _____ times

How many trucks do you need? _____ trucks

Write the division sentence: 20 ÷ _____ = 5

TEACHER NOTES: Equal Groups

(Diagnostic Test Part II: Test Items 6–10)

Making equal groups is a strategy that will help students see the relationship between multiplication and division. Use examples like the ones below to connect the concepts of multiplication and division.

TEACHING ACTIVITIES

Demonstrate the following examples on the board.

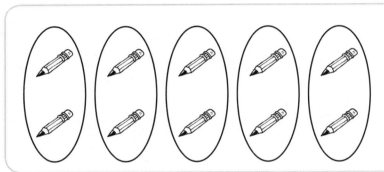

How many groups of 2 = 10?

$10 \div 2 =$ _____

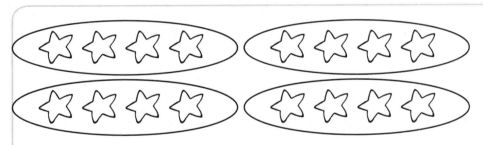

_____ x 4 = 16

$16 \div 4 =$ _____

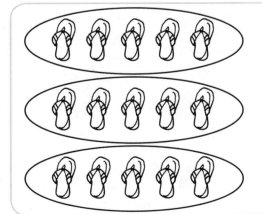

Write a multiplication and a division sentence for the model.

_____ x _____ = _____

_____ ÷ _____ = _____

"One for Me, One for You" (Equal Groups)

Draw on students' experiences with sharing items equally between friends: one for me, one for you. Give students the following problems. Use base ten blocks or other manipulatives to represent the total number of objects in each problem.

Ask students to think of sharing while they solve the problems below. They should write how many each person has, the division sentence, and a corresponding multiplication sentence.

1. 4 circles

    2 friends

    Each friend has _____.

    $4 \div 2 =$ _____

    $2 \times$ _____ $=$ _____

2. 10 hearts

    5 friends

    Each friend has _____.

    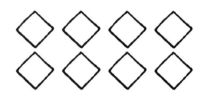

    $10 \div 5 =$ _____

    $5 \times$ _____ $=$ _____

3. 8 diamonds

    4 friends

    Each friend has _____.

    $8 \div 4 =$ _____

    $4 \times$ _____ $=$ _____

4. 12 triangles

    4 friends

    Each friend has _____.

    $12 \div 4 =$ _____

    $4 \times$ _____ $=$ _____

5. 6 moons

    3 friends

    Each friend has _____.

    $6 \div 3 =$ _____

    $3 \times$ _____ $=$ _____

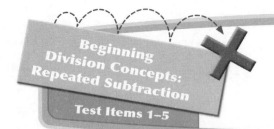

Beginning
Division Concepts:
Repeated Subtraction
Test Items 1–5

Subtract, Subtract, Subtract

Directions: Study the example. Then, use repeated subtraction to find the number of equal groups. Finally, write the matching division sentence.

Example: Use repeated subtraction to find the number of equal groups.

$$12 - 4 = 8 \qquad 8 - 4 = 4 \qquad 4 - 4 = 0$$

Subtracting 4s makes 3 groups, so **12 ÷ 4 = 3**.

1.

Subtract groups of 3.
How many groups? _____
Write the division sentence.

_____

2.

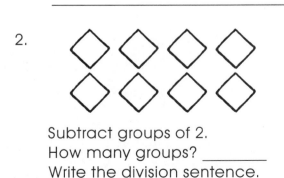

Subtract groups of 2.
How many groups? _____
Write the division sentence.

_____

3.

Subtract groups of 4.
How many groups? _____
Write the division sentence.

_____

4.

Subtract groups of 2.
How many groups? _____
Write the division sentence.

_____

CD-104225 • Jump Into Math • © Carson-Dellosa

More Division by Subtracting

Directions: Use repeated subtraction to find the number of equal groups. Then, write the matching division sentence.

1.

Subtract groups of 3.
How many groups? _____
Write a division sentence.

_____

2.

Subtract groups of 6.
How many groups? _____
Write a division sentence.

_____

3.

Subtract groups of 4.
How many groups? _____
Write a division sentence.

_____

4.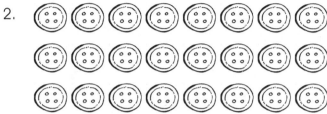

Subtract groups of 5.
How many groups? _____
Write a division sentence.

_____

5.

Subtract groups of 4.
How many groups? _____
Write a division sentence.

_____

6.

Subtract groups of 2.
How many groups? _____
Write a division sentence.

NAME: _____ DATE: _____

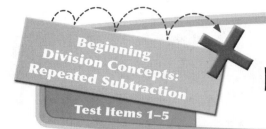

Division Word Problems

Directions: Solve each division word problem by subtracting equal groups. Then write the division sentence for each problem.

1. There are 20 desks in the room.
   Subtract equal groups of 5.
   How many equal groups? _____
   Write the division sentence.

   _____

2. There are 24 candy bars in all.
   Subtract equal groups of 8.
   How many equal groups? _____
   Write the division sentence.

   _____

3. There are 40 pencils in all.
   Subtract equal groups of 10.
   How many equal groups? _____
   Write the division sentence.

   _____

4. There are 36 crayons in all.
   Subtract equal groups of 6.
   How many equal groups? _____
   Write the division sentence.

   _____

5. There are 28 rulers in all.
   Subtract equal groups of 4.
   How many equal groups? _____
   Write the division sentence.

   _____

6. There are 18 marbles in all.
   Subtract equal groups of 3.
   How many equal groups? _____
   Write the division sentence.

   _____

7. There are 20 CDs in all.
   Subtract equal groups of 4.
   How many equal groups? _____
   Write the division sentence.

   _____

8. There are 54 playing cards in all.
   Subtract equal groups of 9.
   How many equal groups? _____
   Write the division sentence.

   _____

CD-104225 • Jump Into Math • © Carson-Dellosa

Making Equal Groups

Directions: Study the example below. For each problem, separate into equal groups. Then, write the division sentence.

Example:

8 blocks

2 equal groups

How many in each group? ___4___

8 ÷ 2 = 4

I.

10 pencils;
5 equal groups.
How many in each group? _____
Write the division sentence.

_____

2.

12 candy bars;
4 equal groups.
How many in each group? _____
Write the division sentence.

_____

3.

15 CDs;
3 equal groups.
How many in each group? _____
Write the division sentence.

_____

4.

18 butterflies;
6 equal groups.
How many in each group? _____
Write the division sentence.

_____

5.

20 desks;
4 equal groups.
How many in each group? _____
Write the division sentence.

_____

6.

24 dogs;
8 equal groups.
How many in each group? _____
Write the division sentence.

_____

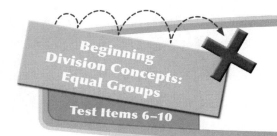

Beginning
Division Concepts:
Equal Groups

Test Items 6–10

An Even Game

Directions: Look at each picture. Circle equal groups and write how many in each group. Then complete the division sentence.

1.

12 footballs
2 groups

_____ in each group   12 ÷ 2 = _____

2.

15 baseballs
3 groups

_____ in each group   15 ÷ 3 = _____

3.

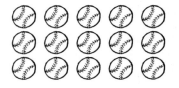

15 soccer balls
5 groups

_____ in each group   15 ÷ 5 = _____

4.

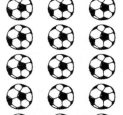

24 basketballs
6 groups

_____ in each group   24 ÷ 6 = _____

CD-104225   •   Jump Into Math   •   © Carson-Dellosa

Fair Shares

Directions: Look at each picture. Circle equal groups and write how many in each group. Then complete the division sentence.

1. 20 squirrels
    4 equal groups

    _____ in each group

    20 ÷ 4 = _____

2. 16 fish
    4 equal groups

    _____ in each group

    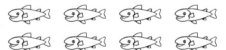

    16 ÷ 4 = _____

3. 15 birds
    3 equal groups

    _____ in each group

    15 ÷ 3 = _____

4. 25 lizards
    5 equal groups

    _____ in each group

    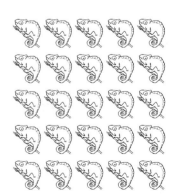

    25 ÷ 5 = _____

Connecting Multiplication and Division

Directions: Write two multiplication sentences and two division sentences to describe each picture.

Example:

$2 \times 4 = 8$ $8 \div 4 = 2$

$4 \times 2 = 8$ $8 \div 2 = 4$

1.

_____ X _____ = _____
_____ X _____ = _____
_____ ÷ _____ = _____
_____ ÷ _____ = _____

2.

_____ X _____ = _____
_____ X _____ = _____
_____ ÷ _____ = _____
_____ ÷ _____ = _____

3.

_____ X _____ = _____
_____ X _____ = _____
_____ ÷ _____ = _____
_____ ÷ _____ = _____

4.

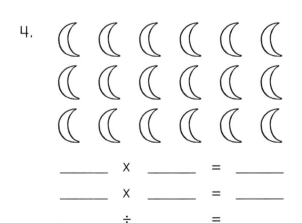

_____ X _____ = _____
_____ X _____ = _____
_____ ÷ _____ = _____
_____ ÷ _____ = _____

CD-104225 • Jump Into Math • © Carson-Dellosa

Matching Multiplication and Division Facts

Directions: Draw a line from each multiplication fact to the matching division fact.

1. 8 x 5 =	A. 10 ÷ 2 =	1. 2 x 6 =	a. 4 ÷ 2 =
2. 7 x 2 =	B. 30 ÷ 5 =	2. 3 x 5 =	b. 35 ÷ 7 =
3. 5 x 1 =	C. 40 ÷ 8 =	3. 2 x 2 =	c. 6 ÷ 3 =
4. 2 x 5 =	D. 8 ÷ 4 =	4. 5 x 10 =	d. 12 ÷ 2 =
5. 2 x 10 =	E. 10 ÷ 5	5. 10 x 1 =	e. 12 ÷ 6 =
6. 4 x 2 =	F. 14 ÷ 7 =	6. 7 x 10 =	f. 10 ÷ 10 =
7. 5 x 6 =	G. 20 ÷ 2 =	7. 3 x 2 =	g. 50 ÷ 5 =
8. 5 x 2 =	H. 20 ÷ 5 =	8. 1 x 5 =	h. 15 ÷ 3 =
9. 9 x 2 =	I. 5 ÷ 5 =	9. 7 x 5 =	i. 70 ÷ 7 =
10. 5 x 4 =	J. 18 ÷ 9 =	10. 6 x 2 =	j. 5 ÷ 1 =

Diagnostic Test:
Multiplication and Division

Directions: Solve each problem in the space provided.

Part III: Multiplication Facts

1. $\begin{array}{r} 2 \\ \times\ 5 \\ \hline \end{array}$

2. $\begin{array}{r} 6 \\ \times\ 2 \\ \hline \end{array}$

3. $\begin{array}{r} 3 \\ \times\ 6 \\ \hline \end{array}$

4. $\begin{array}{r} 10 \\ \times\ 3 \\ \hline \end{array}$

5. $\begin{array}{r} 4 \\ \times\ 8 \\ \hline \end{array}$

6. $\begin{array}{r} 9 \\ \times\ 4 \\ \hline \end{array}$

7. $\begin{array}{r} 6 \\ \times\ 7 \\ \hline \end{array}$

8. $\begin{array}{r} 8 \\ \times\ 6 \\ \hline \end{array}$

9. $\begin{array}{r} 9 \\ \times\ 9 \\ \hline \end{array}$

10. $\begin{array}{r} 10 \\ \times\ 9 \\ \hline \end{array}$

11. 4
  x 2

12. 2
  x 7

13. 5
  x 3

14. 3
  x 8

15. 7
  x 4

16. 5
  x 5

17. 6
  x 6

18. 6
  x 9

19. 9
  x 8

20. 7
  x 1

TEACHER ASSESSMENT AREA

Directions: Shade the boxes that correspond to correct test items.

Skill	Item Number									
Multiplication Facts	1	2	3	4	5	6	7	8	9	10
	11	12	13	14	15	16	17	18	19	20

TOTAL CORRECT: _____

Teacher Notes and Activities

Background Information

Many students experience difficulty solving and answering multiplication facts. Much of this difficulty is often caused by the lack of developmental work preceding fact memorization. If students are successful in the "Beginning Multiplication Concepts" section, they will build the foundation necessary to memorize basic multiplication facts.

TEACHER NOTES: Multiplication Facts

(Diagnostic Test Part I: Test Items 1–20)

Memorization of mathematics facts is very difficult for some students. Instruction must be organized into small, systematic steps. The number of facts that must be memorized can be greatly reduced if you follow the suggested sequence presented below.

TEACHING ACTIVITIES

The following activities constitute a systematic approach to memorizing the basic multiplication facts. Provide students with sufficient practice, including mental math, written practice, rhyming mnemonics, and speed drills. Give each student a blank multiplication chart so that she can fill in the facts as she learns them.

"The Zero Facts" (Multiplication Facts)

Review that multiplication is repeated addition: $0 \times 4 = 0 + 0 + 0 + 0$.

Review that because of the Commutative Property of Multiplication, the order of the factors does not matter: $0 \times 4 = 4 \times 0$.

Remind students that any number multiplied by 0 is 0.

Use the multiplication chart below to review the zero facts with students.

The Zero Facts

x	0	1	2	3	4	5	6	7	8	9
0	0	0	0	0	0	0	0	0	0	0
1	0	1	2	3	4	5	6	7	8	9
2	0	2	4	6	8	10	12	14	16	18
3	0	3	6	9	12	15	18	21	24	27
4	0	4	8	12	16	20	24	28	32	36
5	0	5	10	15	20	25	30	35	40	45
6	0	6	12	18	24	30	36	42	48	54
7	0	7	14	21	28	35	42	49	56	63
8	0	8	16	24	32	40	48	56	64	72
9	0	9	18	27	36	45	54	63	72	81

"The Ones Facts" (Multiplication Facts)

The ones facts also follow the rules of repeated addition and the Commutative Property of Multiplication. Remind students that any number multiplied by 1 is that number.

$$1 \times 5 = 1 + 1 + 1 + 1 + 1$$
$$1 \times 5 = 5 \times 1$$

Students should add the ones facts to their multiplication charts.

x	0	1	2	3	4	5	6	7	8	9
0	0	0	0	0	0	0	0	0	0	0
1	0	1	2	3	4	5	6	7	8	9
2	0	2	4	6	8	10	12	14	16	18
3	0	3	6	9	12	15	18	21	24	27
4	0	4	8	12	16	20	24	28	32	36
5	0	5	10	15	20	25	30	35	40	45
6	0	6	12	18	24	30	36	42	48	54
7	0	7	14	21	28	35	42	49	56	63
8	0	8	16	24	32	40	48	56	64	72
9	0	9	18	27	36	45	54	63	72	81

Once students have learned the 0s and 1s facts, 36 of the 100 facts are memorized!

"The Doubles Facts" (Multiplication Facts)

Many students find it easy to learn the doubles facts: 1 x 1, 2 x 2, 3 x 3, etc. Instruct students to practice the doubles facts and add them to their multiplication charts.

"The Doubles Facts"

x	0	1	2	3	4	5	6	7	8	9
0	0	0	0	0	0	0	0	0	0	0
1	0	1	2	3	4	5	6	7	8	9
2	0	2	4	6	8	10	12	14	16	18
3	0	3	6	9	12	15	18	21	24	27
4	0	4	8	12	16	20	24	28	32	36
5	0	5	10	15	20	25	30	35	40	45
6	0	6	12	18	24	30	36	42	48	54
7	0	7	14	21	28	35	42	49	56	63
8	0	8	16	24	32	40	48	56	64	72
9	0	9	18	27	36	45	54	63	72	81

By learning the 10 doubles facts, students will now know 46 multiplication facts!

"The Two and Five Facts" (Multiplication Facts)

If students have mastered skip counting by 2s and 5s, a quick review will help them to memorize these facts. Instruct students to add them to their multiplication charts.

"The Twos and Fives Facts"

x	0	1	2	3	4	5	6	7	8	9
0	0	0	0	0	0	0	0	0	0	0
1	0	1	2	3	4	5	6	7	8	9
2	0	2	4	6	8	10	12	14	16	18
3	0	3	6	9	12	15	18	21	24	27
4	0	4	8	12	16	20	24	28	32	36
5	0	5	10	15	20	25	30	35	40	45
6	0	6	12	18	24	30	36	42	48	54
7	0	7	14	21	28	35	42	49	56	63
8	0	8	16	24	32	40	48	56	64	72
9	0	9	18	27	36	45	54	63	72	81

"The Nines Facts" (Multiplication Facts)

Introduce the nines facts with the method shown below.

9 x 5

Subtract 1 from the number you are multiplying 9 by (5 – 1 = 4). The first digit in the answer is 4. The sum of the digits in the answer must equal 9. Because 9 - 4 = 5, 5 is the second digit in the answer.

9 x 5 = 45

"The Nines Facts"

x	0	1	2	3	4	5	6	7	8	9
0	0	0	0	0	0	0	0	0	0	0
1	0	1	2	3	4	5	6	7	8	9
2	0	2	4	6	8	10	12	14	16	18
3	0	3	6	9	12	15	18	21	24	27
4	0	4	8	12	16	20	24	28	32	36
5	0	5	10	15	20	25	30	35	40	45
6	0	6	12	18	24	30	36	42	48	54
7	0	7	14	21	28	35	42	49	56	63
8	0	8	16	24	32	40	48	56	64	72
9	0	9	18	27	36	45	54	63	72	81

"The Fours Facts" (Multiplication Facts)

The fours facts can be taught as double-doubles. Look at the examples below.

4 x 3

Double the answer you would get if you multiplied by 2 instead of 4.

Think: 2 x 3 = 6. Double the 6: 6 x 2 = 12. So, **4 x 3 = 12.**

4 x 5

Double the answer you would get if you multiplied by 2 instead of 4.

Think: 2 x 5 = 10. Double the 10: 2 x 10 = 20. So, **4 x 5 = 20.**

"The Four Facts"

	0	1	2	3	4	5	6	7	8	9
0	0	0	0	0	0	0	0	0	0	0
1	0	1	2	3	4	5	6	7	8	9
2	0	2	4	6	8	10	12	14	16	18
3	0	3	6	9	12	15	18	21	24	27
4	0	4	8	12	16	20	24	28	32	36
5	0	5	10	15	20	25	30	35	40	45
6	0	6	12	18	24	30	36	42	48	54
7	0	7	14	21	28	35	42	49	56	63
8	0	8	16	24	32	40	48	56	64	72
9	0	9	18	27	36	45	54	63	72	81

"Mirror Facts: The Commutative Property at Work!" (Multiplication Facts)

Because of the Commutative Property of Multiplication, it is not necessary to memorize 4 x 5 and 5 x 4 separately. The answer is the same for both facts! Teach the facts in the chart that are highlighted. The facts on the other side of the doubles are "mirror facts."

"Mirror Facts"

x	0	1	2	3	4	5	6	7	8	9
0	0	0	0	0	0	0	0	0	0	0
1	0	1	2	3	4	5	6	7	8	9
2	0	2	4	6	8	10	12	14	16	18
3	0	3	6	9	12	15	18	21	24	27
4	0	4	8	12	16	20	24	28	32	36
5	0	5	10	15	20	25	30	35	40	45
6	0	6	12	18	24	30	36	42	48	54
7	0	7	14	21	28	35	42	49	56	63
8	0	8	16	24	32	40	48	56	64	72
9	0	9	18	27	36	45	54	63	72	81

Teach these facts using the commutative property. (That's 28 facts that students will already know!)

"The Final Facts" (Multiplication Facts)

Students' multiplication charts are almost complete. The final facts are shaded in the chart below.

"The Final Facts"

	0	1	2	3	4	5	6	7	8	9
0	0	0	0	0	0	0	0	0	0	0
1	0	1	2	3	4	5	6	7	8	9
2	0	2	4	6	8	10	12	14	16	18
3	0	3	6	9	12	15	18	21	24	27
4	0	4	8	12	16	20	24	28	32	36
5	0	5	10	15	20	25	30	35	40	45
6	0	6	12	18	24	30	36	42	48	54
7	0	7	14	21	28	35	42	49	56	63
8	0	8	16	24	32	40	48	56	64	72
9	0	9	18	27	36	45	54	63	72	81

Use the Commutative Property of Multiplication to teach the remaining 12 facts.

6 x 3	3 x 6
7 x 3	3 x 7
8 x 3	3 x 8
7 x 6	6 x 7
8 x 6	6 x 8
8 x 7	6 x 8

Allow students to practice the basic multiplication facts every day for at least 10 minutes. Speed drills, flash cards, and multiplication games are excellent techniques that lead to computational fluency with the basic multiplication facts.

Multiply by 2

Directions: Use skip counting to help you find each product.

> Skip counting can help you multiply by 2.
>
> Count by 2s: 2, 4, 6, 8, 10, 12, 14, 16, 18, 20

1. 2 x 4 = _____

2.   2
       x 9

3. 4 x 2 = _____

4.   9
       x 2

5. 2 x 3 = _____

6.   2
       x 8

7. 3 x 2 = _____

8.   8
       x 2

9.   2
       x 2

10. 2 x 7 = _____

11.   6
       x 2

12. 1 x 2 = _____

13.   2
       x 1

14. 2 x 0 = _____

15.   2
       x 5

16. 10 x 2 = _____

Multiply by 5

Multiplication Facts

Test Items 1–20

Directions: Use skip counting to help you find each product.

> Skip Counting can help you multiply by 5.
>
> Count by 5s: 5, 10, 15, 20, 25, 30, 35, 40, 45, 50

1. 5 x 4 = _____

2. $\begin{array}{r} 5 \\ \times\ 9 \\ \hline \end{array}$

3. 4 x 5 = _____

4. $\begin{array}{r} 9 \\ \times\ 5 \\ \hline \end{array}$

5. 5 x 3 = _____

6. $\begin{array}{r} 5 \\ \times\ 8 \\ \hline \end{array}$

7. 3 x 5 = _____

8. $\begin{array}{r} 8 \\ \times\ 5 \\ \hline \end{array}$

9. $\begin{array}{r} 5 \\ \times\ 2 \\ \hline \end{array}$

10. 5 x 7 = _____

11. $\begin{array}{r} 6 \\ \times\ 5 \\ \hline \end{array}$

12. 1 x 5 = _____

13. $\begin{array}{r} 5 \\ \times\ 1 \\ \hline \end{array}$

14. 5 x 0 = _____

15. $\begin{array}{r} 5 \\ \times\ 5 \\ \hline \end{array}$

16. 10 x 5 = _____

5s in a Flash

Directions: Cut out each box. Then, find the products. Write each answer on the back of its card. Use the flash cards to practice the 5s facts.

1.
$$\begin{array}{r} 5 \\ \times\ 1 \\ \hline \end{array}$$

2.
$$\begin{array}{r} 5 \\ \times\ 7 \\ \hline \end{array}$$

3.
$$\begin{array}{r} 3 \\ \times\ 5 \\ \hline \end{array}$$

4.
$$\begin{array}{r} 6 \\ \times\ 5 \\ \hline \end{array}$$

5.
$$\begin{array}{r} 2 \\ \times\ 5 \\ \hline \end{array}$$

6.
$$\begin{array}{r} 4 \\ \times\ 5 \\ \hline \end{array}$$

7.
$$\begin{array}{r} 5 \\ \times\ 8 \\ \hline \end{array}$$

8.
$$\begin{array}{r} 9 \\ \times\ 5 \\ \hline \end{array}$$

9.
$$\begin{array}{r} 5 \\ \times\ 10 \\ \hline \end{array}$$

10.
$$\begin{array}{r} 5 \\ \times\ 4 \\ \hline \end{array}$$

11.
$$\begin{array}{r} 5 \\ \times\ 5 \\ \hline \end{array}$$

12.
$$\begin{array}{r} 0 \\ \times\ 5 \\ \hline \end{array}$$

CD-104225 • Jump Into Math • © Carson-Dellosa

Multiplying by 10

Multiplication Facts

Test Items 1–20

Directions: Use skip counting to help find each product.

> Use the 1s facts and skip counting to help you multiply by 10.
>
> Count by 10s: 10, 20, 30, 40, 50, 60, 70, 80, 90, 100

1. 1 x 5 = _____

   10 x 5 = _____

2. 1 x 3 = _____

   10 x 3 = _____

3. 1 x 8 = _____

   10 x 8 = _____

4. 1 x 4 = _____

   10 x 4 = _____

5. 1 x 0 = _____

   10 x 0 = _____

6. 1 x 2 = _____

   10 x 2 = _____

7. 1 x 6 = _____

   10 x 6 = _____

8. 1 x 7 = _____

   10 x 7 = _____

9. 1 x 1 = _____

   10 x 1 = _____

10. 1 x 10 = _____

   10 x 10 = _____

Multiplication Facts

Test Items 1–20

10s in a Flash

Directions: Cut out each box. Then, find the products. Write each answer on the back of its card. Use the flash cards to practice the 10s facts.

1.
$$\begin{array}{r} 10 \\ \times\ 2 \\ \hline \end{array}$$

2.
$$\begin{array}{r} 8 \\ \times\ 10 \\ \hline \end{array}$$

3.
$$\begin{array}{r} 10 \\ \times\ 3 \\ \hline \end{array}$$

4.
$$\begin{array}{r} 1 \\ \times\ 10 \\ \hline \end{array}$$

5.
$$\begin{array}{r} 10 \\ \times\ 8 \\ \hline \end{array}$$

6.
$$\begin{array}{r} 0 \\ \times\ 10 \\ \hline \end{array}$$

7.
$$\begin{array}{r} 10 \\ \times\ 7 \\ \hline \end{array}$$

8.
$$\begin{array}{r} 9 \\ \times\ 10 \\ \hline \end{array}$$

9.
$$\begin{array}{r} 10 \\ \times\ 4 \\ \hline \end{array}$$

10.
$$\begin{array}{r} 10 \\ \times\ 10 \\ \hline \end{array}$$

11.
$$\begin{array}{r} 10 \\ \times\ 6 \\ \hline \end{array}$$

12.
$$\begin{array}{r} 5 \\ \times\ 10 \\ \hline \end{array}$$

CD-104225 • Jump Into Math • © Carson-Dellosa

3s in a Flash

Multiplication Facts

Test Items 1–20

Directions: Cut out each box. Then, find the products. Write each answer on the back of its card. Use the flash cards to practice the 3s facts.

1.
$$\begin{array}{r} 3 \\ \times\ 2 \\ \hline \end{array}$$

2.
$$\begin{array}{r} 8 \\ \times\ 3 \\ \hline \end{array}$$

3.
$$\begin{array}{r} 1 \\ \times\ 3 \\ \hline \end{array}$$

4.
$$\begin{array}{r} 3 \\ \times\ 5 \\ \hline \end{array}$$

5.
$$\begin{array}{r} 3 \\ \times\ 7 \\ \hline \end{array}$$

6.
$$\begin{array}{r} 0 \\ \times\ 3 \\ \hline \end{array}$$

7.
$$\begin{array}{r} 3 \\ \times\ 4 \\ \hline \end{array}$$

8.
$$\begin{array}{r} 3 \\ \times\ 3 \\ \hline \end{array}$$

9.
$$\begin{array}{r} 3 \\ \times\ 10 \\ \hline \end{array}$$

10.
$$\begin{array}{r} 3 \\ \times\ 6 \\ \hline \end{array}$$

11.
$$\begin{array}{r} 9 \\ \times\ 3 \\ \hline \end{array}$$

12.
$$\begin{array}{r} 3 \\ \times\ 8 \\ \hline \end{array}$$

4s in a Flash

Directions: Cut out each box. Then, find the products. Write each answer on the back of its card. Use the flash cards to practice the 4s facts.

1.
$$\begin{array}{r} 4 \\ \times\ 1 \\ \hline \end{array}$$

2.
$$\begin{array}{r} 4 \\ \times\ 7 \\ \hline \end{array}$$

3.
$$\begin{array}{r} 3 \\ \times\ 4 \\ \hline \end{array}$$

4.
$$\begin{array}{r} 6 \\ \times\ 4 \\ \hline \end{array}$$

5.
$$\begin{array}{r} 2 \\ \times\ 4 \\ \hline \end{array}$$

6.
$$\begin{array}{r} 4 \\ \times\ 4 \\ \hline \end{array}$$

7.
$$\begin{array}{r} 4 \\ \times\ 8 \\ \hline \end{array}$$

8.
$$\begin{array}{r} 9 \\ \times\ 4 \\ \hline \end{array}$$

9.
$$\begin{array}{r} 4 \\ \times\ 10 \\ \hline \end{array}$$

10.
$$\begin{array}{r} 7 \\ \times\ 4 \\ \hline \end{array}$$

11.
$$\begin{array}{r} 4 \\ \times\ 5 \\ \hline \end{array}$$

12.
$$\begin{array}{r} 0 \\ \times\ 4 \\ \hline \end{array}$$

CD-104225 • Jump Into Math • © Carson-Dellosa

6s in a Flash

Multiplication Facts

Test Items 1–20

Directions: Cut out each box. Then, find the products. Write each answer on the back of its card. Use the flash cards to practice the 6s facts.

1.

$$\begin{array}{r} 6 \\ \times\ 1 \\ \hline \end{array}$$

2.

$$\begin{array}{r} 6 \\ \times\ 7 \\ \hline \end{array}$$

3.

$$\begin{array}{r} 3 \\ \times\ 6 \\ \hline \end{array}$$

4.

$$\begin{array}{r} 6 \\ \times\ 6 \\ \hline \end{array}$$

5.

$$\begin{array}{r} 2 \\ \times\ 6 \\ \hline \end{array}$$

6.

$$\begin{array}{r} 4 \\ \times\ 6 \\ \hline \end{array}$$

7.

$$\begin{array}{r} 6 \\ \times\ 8 \\ \hline \end{array}$$

8.

$$\begin{array}{r} 9 \\ \times\ 6 \\ \hline \end{array}$$

9.

$$\begin{array}{r} 6 \\ \times\ 10 \\ \hline \end{array}$$

10.

$$\begin{array}{r} 7 \\ \times\ 6 \\ \hline \end{array}$$

11.

$$\begin{array}{r} 6 \\ \times\ 5 \\ \hline \end{array}$$

12.

$$\begin{array}{r} 0 \\ \times\ 6 \\ \hline \end{array}$$

7s in a Flash

Directions: Cut out each box. Then, find the products. Write each answer on the back of its card. Use the flash cards to practice the 7s facts.

1.

$$\begin{array}{r} 7 \\ \times\ 1 \\ \hline \end{array}$$

2.

$$\begin{array}{r} 4 \\ \times\ 7 \\ \hline \end{array}$$

3.

$$\begin{array}{r} 3 \\ \times\ 7 \\ \hline \end{array}$$

4.

$$\begin{array}{r} 6 \\ \times\ 7 \\ \hline \end{array}$$

5.

$$\begin{array}{r} 2 \\ \times\ 7 \\ \hline \end{array}$$

6.

$$\begin{array}{r} 5 \\ \times\ 7 \\ \hline \end{array}$$

7.

$$\begin{array}{r} 7 \\ \times\ 8 \\ \hline \end{array}$$

8.

$$\begin{array}{r} 9 \\ \times\ 7 \\ \hline \end{array}$$

9.

$$\begin{array}{r} 7 \\ \times\ 10 \\ \hline \end{array}$$

10.

$$\begin{array}{r} 7 \\ \times\ 7 \\ \hline \end{array}$$

11.

$$\begin{array}{r} 7 \\ \times\ 5 \\ \hline \end{array}$$

12.

$$\begin{array}{r} 0 \\ \times\ 7 \\ \hline \end{array}$$

CD-104225 • Jump Into Math • © Carson-Dellosa

8s in a Flash

Directions: Cut out each box. Then, find the products. Write each answer on the back of its card. Use the flash cards to practice the 8s facts.

1.
$$\begin{array}{r} 8 \\ \times\ 1 \\ \hline \end{array}$$

2.
$$\begin{array}{r} 8 \\ \times\ 7 \\ \hline \end{array}$$

3.
$$\begin{array}{r} 3 \\ \times\ 8 \\ \hline \end{array}$$

4.
$$\begin{array}{r} 8 \\ \times\ 6 \\ \hline \end{array}$$

5.
$$\begin{array}{r} 2 \\ \times\ 8 \\ \hline \end{array}$$

6.
$$\begin{array}{r} 4 \\ \times\ 8 \\ \hline \end{array}$$

7.
$$\begin{array}{r} 8 \\ \times\ 8 \\ \hline \end{array}$$

8.
$$\begin{array}{r} 9 \\ \times\ 8 \\ \hline \end{array}$$

9.
$$\begin{array}{r} 8 \\ \times\ 10 \\ \hline \end{array}$$

10.
$$\begin{array}{r} 7 \\ \times\ 8 \\ \hline \end{array}$$

11.
$$\begin{array}{r} 8 \\ \times\ 5 \\ \hline \end{array}$$

12.
$$\begin{array}{r} 0 \\ \times\ 8 \\ \hline \end{array}$$

NAME: _____ DATE: _____

Multiplication Facts

Test Items 1–20

9s in a Flash

Directions: Cut out each box. Then, find the products. Write each answer on the back of its card. Use the flash cards to practice the 9s facts.

1.
$$\begin{array}{r} 9 \\ \times\ 1 \\ \hline \end{array}$$

2.
$$\begin{array}{r} 4 \\ \times\ 9 \\ \hline \end{array}$$

3.
$$\begin{array}{r} 3 \\ \times\ 9 \\ \hline \end{array}$$

4.
$$\begin{array}{r} 6 \\ \times\ 9 \\ \hline \end{array}$$

5.
$$\begin{array}{r} 2 \\ \times\ 9 \\ \hline \end{array}$$

6.
$$\begin{array}{r} 5 \\ \times\ 9 \\ \hline \end{array}$$

7.
$$\begin{array}{r} 9 \\ \times\ 8 \\ \hline \end{array}$$

8.
$$\begin{array}{r} 9 \\ \times\ 9 \\ \hline \end{array}$$

9.
$$\begin{array}{r} 9 \\ \times\ 10 \\ \hline \end{array}$$

10.
$$\begin{array}{r} 9 \\ \times\ 7 \\ \hline \end{array}$$

11.
$$\begin{array}{r} 9 \\ \times\ 5 \\ \hline \end{array}$$

12.
$$\begin{array}{r} 0 \\ \times\ 9 \\ \hline \end{array}$$

Speed Drill: 2s Facts

Multiplication Facts

Test Items 1–20

Directions: Multiply. Write your answer to each problem.

1. 2 x 9 = _____

2. 2 x 2 = _____

3. 2 x 3 = _____

4. 2 x 8 = _____

5. 2 x 7 = _____

6. 2 x 1 = _____

7. 2 x 4 = _____

8. 2 x 10 = _____

9. 2 x 0 = _____

10. 2 x 6 = _____

11. 2 x 9 = _____

12. 2 x 10 = _____

13. 2 x 2 = _____

14. 2 x 5 = _____

15. 2 x 3 = _____

16. 2 x 4 = _____

17. 2 x 6 = _____

18. 2 x 8 = _____

19. 2 x 7 = _____

20. 2 x 10 = _____

21. 2 x 4 = _____

22. 2 x 1 = _____

23. 2 x 6 = _____

24. 2 x 7 = _____

25. 2 x 8 = _____

26. 2 x 0 = _____

27. 2 x 3 = _____

28. 2 x 9 = _____

29. 2 x 6 = _____

30. 2 x 3 = _____

31. 2 x 5 = _____

32. 2 x 8 = _____

33. 2 x 9 = _____

34. 2 x 7 = _____

35. 2 x 4 = _____

36. 2 x 2 = _____

Speed Drill: 3s Facts

Multiplication Facts

Test Items 1–20

Directions: Multiply. Write your answer to each problem.

1. 3 x 9 = _____	10. 3 x 6 = _____	19. 3 x 7 = _____	28. 3 x 9 = _____
2. 3 x 3 = _____	11. 3 x 2 = _____	20. 3 x 10 = _____	29. 3 x 6 = _____
3. 3 x 2 = _____	12. 3 x 10 = _____	21. 3 x 0 = _____	30. 3 x 3 = _____
4. 3 x 8 = _____	13. 3 x 2 = _____	22. 3 x 1 = _____	31. 3 x 5 = _____
5. 3 x 7 = _____	14. 3 x 5 = _____	23. 3 x 6 = _____	32. 3 x 8 = _____
6. 3 x 1 = _____	15. 3 x 3 = _____	24. 3 x 7 = _____	33. 3 x 9 = _____
7. 3 x 4 = _____	16. 3 x 4 = _____	25. 3 x 8 = _____	34. 3 x 7 = _____
8. 3 x 8 = _____	17. 3 x 6 = _____	26. 3 x 6 = _____	35. 3 x 4 = _____
9. 3 x 0 = _____	18. 3 x 8 = _____	27. 3 x 3 = _____	36. 3 x 2 = _____

CD-104225 • Jump Into Math • © Carson-Dellosa

Speed Drill: 4s Facts

Multiplication Facts

Test Items 1–20

Directions: Multiply. Write your answer to each problem.

1. 4 x 9 = _____	10. 4 x 6 = _____	19. 4 x 7 = _____	28. 4 x 9 = _____
2. 4 x 2 = _____	11. 4 x 2 = _____	20. 4 x 10 = _____	29. 4 x 6 = _____
3. 4 x 3 = _____	12. 4 x 10 = _____	21. 4 x 4 = _____	30. 4 x 3 = _____
4. 4 x 8 = _____	13. 4 x 4 = _____	22. 4 x 1 = _____	31. 4 x 5 = _____
5. 4 x 7 = _____	14. 4 x 5 = _____	23. 4 x 6 = _____	32. 4 x 8 = _____
6. 4 x 1 = _____	15. 4 x 3 = _____	24. 4 x 7 = _____	33. 4 x 9 = _____
7. 4 x 4 = _____	16. 4 x 2 = _____	25. 4 x 8 = _____	34. 4 x 7 = _____
8. 4 x 8 = _____	17. 4 x 6 = _____	26. 4 x 6 = _____	35. 4 x 4 = _____
9. 4 x 0 = _____	18. 4 x 8 = _____	27. 4 x 3 = _____	36. 4 x 2 = _____

NAME: _____ DATE: _____

Speed Drill: 5s Facts

Directions: Multiply. Write your answer to each problem.

1. 5 x 9 = _____
2. 5 x 2 = _____
3. 5 x 3 = _____
4. 5 x 8 = _____
5. 5 x 7 = _____
6. 5 x 1 = _____
7. 5 x 4 = _____
8. 5 x 8 = _____
9. 5 x 0 = _____

10. 5 x 6 = _____
11. 5 x 2 = _____
12. 5 x 10 = _____
13. 5 x 4 = _____
14. 5 x 5 = _____
15. 5 x 3 = _____
16. 5 x 2 = _____
17. 5 x 6 = _____
18. 5 x 8 = _____

19. 5 x 7 = _____
20. 5 x 10 = _____
21. 5 x 4 = _____
22. 5 x 1 = _____
23. 5 x 6 = _____
24. 5 x 7 = _____
25. 5 x 8 = _____
26. 5 x 0 = _____
27. 5 x 3 = _____

28. 5 x 9 = _____
29. 5 x 6 = _____
30. 5 x 3 = _____
31. 5 x 5 = _____
32. 5 x 8 = _____
33. 5 x 9 = _____
34. 5 x 7 = _____
35. 5 x 4 = _____
36. 5 x 2 = _____

Speed Drill: 6s Facts

Multiplication Facts

Test Items 1–20

Directions: Multiply. Write your answer to each problem.

1. 6 x 9 = _____	10. 6 x 6 = _____	19. 6 x 7 = _____	28. 6 x 9 = _____
2. 6 x 2 = _____	11. 6 x 2 = _____	20. 6 x 10 = _____	29. 6 x 6 = _____
3. 6 x 3 = _____	12. 6 x 10 = _____	21. 6 x 4 = _____	30. 6 x 3 = _____
4. 6 x 8 = _____	13. 6 x 4 = _____	22. 6 x 1 = _____	31. 6 x 5 = _____
5. 6 x 7 = _____	14. 6 x 5 = _____	23. 6 x 6 = _____	32. 6 x 8 = _____
6. 6 x 1 = _____	15. 6 x 3 = _____	24. 6 x 7 = _____	33. 6 x 9 = _____
7. 6 x 4 = _____	16. 6 x 2 = _____	25. 6 x 8 = _____	34. 6 x 7 = _____
8. 6 x 8 = _____	17. 6 x 6 = _____	26. 6 x 0 = _____	35. 6 x 4 = _____
9. 6 x 0 = _____	18. 6 x 8 = _____	27. 6 x 3 = _____	36. 6 x 2 = _____

Multiplication Facts

Test Items 1–20

Speed Drill: 7s Facts

Directions: Multiply. Write your answer to each problem.

1. 7 x 9 = _____	10. 7 x 6 = _____	19. 7 x 7 = _____	28. 7 x 9 = _____
2. 7 x 2 = _____	11. 7 x 2 = _____	20. 7 x 10 = _____	29. 7 x 6 = _____
3. 7 x 3 = _____	12. 7 x 10 = _____	21. 7 x 4 = _____	30. 7 x 3 = _____
4. 7 x 8 = _____	13. 7 x 4 = _____	22. 7 x 1 = _____	31. 7 x 5 = _____
5. 7 x 7 = _____	14. 7 x 5 = _____	23. 7 x 6 = _____	32. 7 x 8 = _____
6. 7 x 1 = _____	15. 7 x 3 = _____	24. 7 x 7 = _____	33. 7 x 9 = _____
7. 7 x 4 = _____	16. 7 x 2 = _____	25. 7 x 8 = _____	34. 7 x 7 = _____
8. 7 x 8 = _____	17. 7 x 6 = _____	26. 7 x 0 = _____	35. 7 x 4 = _____
9. 7 x 0 = _____	18. 7 x 8 = _____	27. 7 x 3 = _____	36. 7 x 2 = _____

CD-104225 • Jump Into Math • © Carson-Dellosa

Speed Drill: 8s Facts

Multiplication Facts

Test Items 1–20

Directions: Multiply. Write your answer to each problem.

1. 8 x 9 = _____	10. 8 x 6 = _____	19. 8 x 7 = _____	28. 8 x 9 = _____
2. 8 x 2 = _____	11. 8 x 2 = _____	20. 8 x 10 = _____	29. 8 x 6 = _____
3. 8 x 3 = _____	12. 8 x 10 = _____	21. 8 x 4 = _____	30. 8 x 3 = _____
4. 8 x 8 = _____	13. 8 x 4 = _____	22. 8 x 1 = _____	31. 8 x 5 = _____
5. 8 x 7 = _____	14. 8 x 5 = _____	23. 8 x 6 = _____	32. 8 x 8 = _____
6. 8 x 1 = _____	15. 8 x 3 = _____	24. 8 x 7 = _____	33. 8 x 9 = _____
7. 8 x 4 = _____	16. 8 x 2 = _____	25. 8 x 8 = _____	34. 8 x 7 = _____
8. 8 x 8 = _____	17. 8 x 6 = _____	26. 8 x 0 = _____	35. 8 x 4 = _____
9. 8 x 0 = _____	18. 8 x 8 = _____	27. 8 x 3 = _____	36. 8 x 2 = _____

Speed Drill: 9s Facts

Directions: Multiply. Write your answer to each problem.

1. 9 x 9 = _____

2. 9 x 2 = _____

3. 9 x 3 = _____

4. 9 x 8 = _____

5. 9 x 7 = _____

6. 9 x 1 = _____

7. 9 x 4 = _____

8. 9 x 8 = _____

9. 9 x 0 = _____

10. 9 x 6 = _____

11. 9 x 2 = _____

12. 9 x 10 = _____

13. 9 x 4 = _____

14. 9 x 5 = _____

15. 9 x 3 = _____

16. 9 x 2 = _____

17. 9 x 6 = _____

18. 9 x 8 = _____

19. 9 x 7 = _____

20. 9 x 10 = _____

21. 9 x 4 = _____

22. 9 x 1 = _____

23. 9 x 6 = _____

24. 9 x 7 = _____

25. 9 x 8 = _____

26. 9 x 0 = _____

27. 9 x 3 = _____

28. 9 x 9 = _____

29. 9 x 6 = _____

30. 9 x 3 = _____

31. 9 x 5 = _____

32. 9 x 8 = _____

33. 9 x 9 = _____

34. 9 x 7 = _____

35. 9 x 4 = _____

36. 9 x 2 = _____

CD-104225 • Jump Into Math • © Carson-Dellosa

Speed Drill: Mixed Facts

Multiplication Facts

Test Items 1–20

Directions: Multiply. Write your answer to each problem.

1. 9 x 8 = _____
2. 6 x 2 = _____
3. 4 x 1 = _____
4. 8 x 5 = _____
5. 3 x 9 = _____
6. 5 x 3 = _____
7. 10 x 6 = _____
8. 2 x 7 = _____
9. 7 x 4 = _____

10. 1 x 6 = _____
11. 7 x 2 = _____
12. 6 x 8 = _____
13. 7 x 7 = _____
14. 0 x 3 = _____
15. 8 x 4 = _____
16. 4 x 10 = _____
17. 9 x 1 = _____
18. 3 x 2 = _____

19. 5 x 5 = _____
20. 2 x 9 = _____
21. 5 x 4 = _____
22. 3 x 7 = _____
23. 1 x 2 = _____
24. 6 x 7 = _____
25. 9 x 8 = _____
26. 8 x 1 = _____
27. 4 x 3 = _____

28. 9 x 9 = _____
29. 3 x 6 = _____
30. 6 x 3 = _____
31. 5 x 5 = _____
32. 4 x 8 = _____
33. 2 x 9 = _____
34. 1 x 7 = _____
35. 0 x 4 = _____
36. 8 x 2 = _____

Speed Drill:
More Mixed Facts

Directions: Multiply. Write your answer to each problem.

1. 9 x 3 = _____

2. 6 x 1 = _____

3. 4 x 5 = _____

4. 8 x 8 = _____

5. 3 x 0 = _____

6. 5 x 9 = _____

7. 10 x 7 = _____

8. 2 x 6 = _____

9. 7 x 3 = _____

10. 1 x 5 = _____

11. 7 x 4 = _____

12. 6 x 9 = _____

13. 7 x 7 = _____

14. 1 x 2 = _____

15. 8 x 5 = _____

16. 9 x 10 = _____

17. 9 x 8 = _____

18. 3 x 7 = _____

19. 4 x 6 = _____

20. 3 x 8 = _____

21. 6 x 5 = _____

22. 4 x 8 = _____

23. 2 x 3 = _____

24. 7 x 8 = _____

25. 9 x 7 = _____

26. 9 x 2 = _____

27. 5 x 4 = _____

28. 9 x 9 = _____

29. 4 x 7 = _____

30. 7 x 3 = _____

31. 6 x 6 = _____

32. 5 x 9 = _____

33. 3 x 0 = _____

34. 2 x 8 = _____

35. 0 x 5 = _____

36. 9 x 2 = _____

CD-104225 • Jump Into Math • © Carson-Dellosa

Diagnostic Test:
Multiplication and Division

Directions: Write your answer to each question in the space provided.

Part IV: Division Facts

1. $4 \div 2 =$ _____

5. $18 \div 3 =$ _____

2. $3\overline{)12}$

6. $5\overline{)35}$

3. $12 \div 2 =$ _____

7. $27 \div 3 =$ _____

4. $5\overline{)45}$

8. $4\overline{)36}$

9. $81 \div 9 =$ _____

10. $9\overline{)0}$

11. $54 \div 6 =$ _____

12. $7\overline{)49}$

13. $40 \div 8 =$ _____

14. $6\overline{)48}$

15. $72 \div 8 =$ _____

TEACHER ASSESSMENT AREA

Directions: Shade the boxes that correspond to correct test items.

Skill	Item Number							
Division Facts	1	2	3	4	5	6	7	8
	9	10	11	12	13	14	15	

TOTAL CORRECT: _____

Teacher Notes and Activities

TEACHER NOTES: Division Fact Strategies
(Diagnostic Test Part II: Test Items 1–15)

Because division is the inverse operation of multiplication, the basic division facts should be taught along with the basic multiplication facts. Through practice with fact families and multiplication tables, students can begin to develop an understanding of the relationship between multiplication and division.

TEACHING ACTIVITIES

"Using the Multiplication Table to Divide" (Division Facts)

Give each student a basic multiplication facts table. Explain this the table can be used to find the missing factor in a division problem. Demonstrate with the example below.

$$72 \div 9 =$$

x	0	1	2	3	4	5	6	7	8	9
0	0	0	0	0	0	0	0	0	0	0
1	0	1	2	3	4	5	6	7	8	9
2	0	2	4	6	8	10	12	14	16	18
3	0	3	6	9	12	15	18	21	24	27
4	0	4	8	12	16	20	24	28	32	36
5	0	5	10	15	20	25	30	35	40	45
6	0	6	12	18	24	30	36	42	48	54
7	0	7	14	21	28	35	42	49	56	63
8	0	8	16	24	32	40	48	56	64	72
9	0	9	18	27	36	45	54	63	72	81

Step 1: Write a missing factor multiplication problem from the division problem: ☐ x 9 = 72.

Step 2: Find the product (72) in the row of the known factor (9).

Step 3: The missing factor is at the top of the products column: 9 x ⌷8⌷ = 72. So, 72 ÷ 9 = 8.

Ask students to solve the following division problems using the multiplication table method.

10 ÷ 2	15 ÷ 3	56 ÷ 8
15 ÷ 5	8 ÷ 4	42 ÷ 6
25 ÷ 5	0 ÷ 5	32 ÷ 8
24 ÷ 3	14 ÷ 2	35 ÷ 7

"Division with Zero and One" (Division Facts)

Teach students that numbers cannot be divided by 0, but when 0 is divided by any other number, the answer is 0.

Provide students with a blank division chart like the one shown below and instruct them to write in the 0 facts.

Show students that any number divided by 1 equals that number. When you divide by 1, you have one group, and everything is in that group.

Instruct students to make a division chart for dividing by 1.

Blank Division Chart

÷	=	
÷	=	
÷	=	
÷	=	
÷	=	
÷	=	
÷	=	
÷	=	
÷	=	
÷	=	

Division Charts for 0 and 1

Dividing 0
0 ÷ 1 = 0
0 ÷ 2 = 0
0 ÷ 3 = 0
0 ÷ 4 = 0
0 ÷ 5 = 0
0 ÷ 6 = 0
0 ÷ 7 = 0
0 ÷ 8 = 0
0 ÷ 9 = 0

Division by 1
0 ÷ 1 = 0
1 ÷ 1 = 1
2 ÷ 1 = 2
3 ÷ 1 = 3
4 ÷ 1 = 4
5 ÷ 1 = 5
6 ÷ 1 = 6
7 ÷ 1 = 7
8 ÷ 1 = 8
9 ÷ 1 = 9

Help students make flash cards for division with 0 and 1. Write the division facts on the front of the cards and the multiplication facts on the back of the cards.

Front

0 ÷ 8 = 0

Back*

8 x 0 = 0

Note: According to the commutative property of multiplication, students can write either 8 x 0 or 0 x 8 on the back of their flash cards for the example above. The same is not true for the division problems with 0 on the fronts of the cards since numbers cannot be divide by 0.

CD-104225 • Jump Into Math • © Carson-Dellosa

"Division by Two and Five" (Division Facts)

Build on students' prior knowledge of skip counting and basic multiplication facts to teach division by 2 and 5.

Division by 2
$0 \div 2 = 0$
$2 \div 2 = 1$
$4 \div 2 = 2$
$6 \div 2 = 3$
$8 \div 2 = 4$
$10 \div 2 = 5$
$12 \div 2 = 6$
$14 \div 2 = 7$
$16 \div 2 = 8$
$18 \div 2 = 9$

Division by 5
$0 \div 5 = 0$
$5 \div 5 = 1$
$10 \div 5 = 2$
$15 \div 5 = 3$
$20 \div 5 = 4$
$25 \div 5 = 5$
$30 \div 5 = 6$
$35 \div 5 = 7$
$40 \div 5 = 8$
$45 \div 5 = 9$

Help students make flash cards for the division and multiplication by 2 and 5 facts.

"Doubles Are No Trouble" (Division Facts)

Explore with students division facts that have identical factors, such as $25 \div 5 = 5$. Practice these division facts until students memorize them. Add these facts to their flash card collections.

Division Doubles
$1 \div 1 = 1$
$4 \div 2 = 2$
$9 \div 3 = 3$
$16 \div 4 = 4$
$25 \div 5 = 5$
$36 \div 6 = 6$
$49 \div 7 = 7$
$64 \div 8 = 8$
$81 \div 9 = 9$

Direct students to find these facts on the basic multiplication facts table. Ask students if they can see a pattern. Demonstrate that doubles facts follow a diagonal line through the table.

"Threes and Fours" (Division Facts)

Introduce the division by 3 and 4 facts. Provide each student with a hundred chart. Direct students to skip count by 3s and 4s, coloring multiples of 3 red and multiples of 4 blue. Then, ask students if there are numbers that should be colored with both red and blue. Help students make flash cards using the division charts below. Repeat the activity using 2s and 5s or 6s, 7s, 8s, and 9s.

Division by 3
$0 \div 3 = 0$
$3 \div 3 = 1$
$6 \div 3 = 2$
$9 \div 3 = 3$
$12 \div 3 = 4$
$15 \div 3 = 5$
$18 \div 3 = 6$
$21 \div 3 = 7$
$24 \div 3 = 8$
$27 \div 3 = 9$

Division by 4
$0 \div 4 = 0$
$4 \div 4 = 1$
$8 \div 4 = 2$
$12 \div 4 = 3$
$16 \div 4 = 4$
$20 \div 4 = 5$
$24 \div 4 = 6$
$28 \div 4 = 7$
$32 \div 4 = 8$
$36 \div 4 = 9$

"Skip Count Backwards" (Division Facts)

Students should practice skip counting backwards by 3s and 4s. Give students number lines beginning and ending with different numbers between 1 and 100. Ask them to count backwards by either 3s or 4s. Look at the examples below.

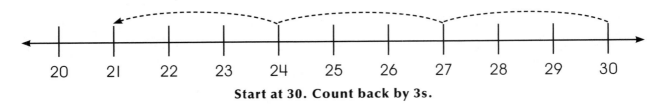

Start at 30. Count back by 3s.

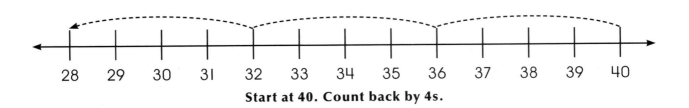

Start at 40. Count back by 4s.

"Sixes, Sevens, Eights, and Nines" (Division Facts)

Rely on the multiplication table to help students review the matching multiplication facts for these division facts. Students should practice finding missing factors in facts. For example, 7 x ☐ = 56. Students should find the missing factors by using the related division facts, such as 56 ÷ 7 = 8 in this example. Also, have students practice by writing two division facts for each multiplication fact. For example, 6 x 9 = 54, so students would write 54 ÷ 6 = 9 and 54 ÷ 9 = 6. Help students complete their flash card sets with these final facts.

Division by 6	Division by 7	Division by 8	Division by 9
0 ÷ 6 = 0	0 ÷ 7 = 0	0 ÷ 8 = 0	0 ÷ 9 = 0
6 ÷ 6 = 1	7 ÷ 7 = 1	8 ÷ 8 = 1	9 ÷ 9 = 1
12 ÷ 6 = 2	14 ÷ 7 = 2	16 ÷ 8 = 2	18 ÷ 9 = 2
18 ÷ 6 = 3	21 ÷ 7 = 3	24 ÷ 8 = 3	27 ÷ 9 = 3
24 ÷ 6 = 4	28 ÷ 7 = 4	32 ÷ 8 = 4	36 ÷ 9 = 4
30 ÷ 6 = 5	35 ÷ 7 = 5	40 ÷ 8 = 5	45 ÷ 9 = 5
36 ÷ 6 = 6	42 ÷ 7 = 6	48 ÷ 8 = 6	54 ÷ 9 = 6
42 ÷ 6 = 7	49 ÷ 7 = 7	56 ÷ 8 = 7	63 ÷ 9 = 7
48 ÷ 6 = 8	56 ÷ 7 = 8	64 ÷ 8 = 8	72 ÷ 9 = 8
54 ÷ 6 = 9	63 ÷ 7 = 9	72 ÷ 8 = 9	81 ÷ 9 = 9

Direct students to work in pairs to practice using their division flash cards. Since each flash card has a division fact on the front and a multiplication fact on the back, instruct students to practice with both operations.

"Bonus Facts!" (Division Facts)

When students are comfortable with the basic division facts, begin teaching the 10s division facts. These facts are easy for students to master because of students' prior experience with place value, skip counting, and basic facts.

Division by 10
0 ÷ 10 = 0
10 ÷ 10 = 1
20 ÷ 10 = 2
30 ÷ 10 = 3
40 ÷ 10 = 4
50 ÷ 10 = 5
60 ÷ 10 = 6
70 ÷ 10 = 7
80 ÷ 10 = 8
90 ÷ 10 = 9

All students must memorize the basic multiplication and division facts. For some, this can take several years. Allow students to keep a multiplication table available for reference as the multiplication and division algorithms are developed, especially when including multi-digit operations.

Divide by 2

Directions: Skip count backward to find each quotient.

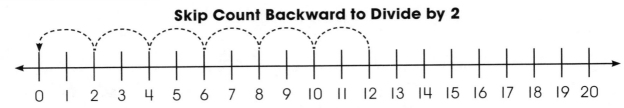

Skip Count Backward to Divide by 2

How many groups of 2 in 12? Count backward from 12. The quotient is 6.

12 ÷ 2 = 6

1. 8 ÷ 2 = _____

2. 18 ÷ 2 = _____

3. 16 ÷ 2 = _____

4. 6 ÷ 2 = _____

5. 4 ÷ 2 = _____

6. 14 ÷ 2 = _____

7. 12 ÷ 2 = _____

8. 2 ÷ 2 = _____

9. 10 ÷ 2 = _____

10. 0 ÷ 2 = _____

CD-104225 • Jump Into Math • © Carson-Dellosa

Divide by 5

Directions: Skip count backward to find each quotient.

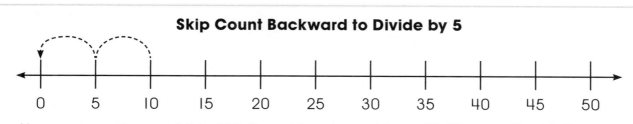

Skip Count Backward to Divide by 5

How many groups of 5 in 10? Count backward from 10. The quotient is 2.

10 ÷ 5 = 2

1. 10 ÷ 5 = _____

2. 25 ÷ 5 = _____

3. 40 ÷ 5 = _____

4. 5 ÷ 5 = _____

5. 15 ÷ 5 = _____

6. 20 ÷ 5 = _____

7. 0 ÷ 5 = _____

8. 30 ÷ 5 = _____

9. 50 ÷ 5 = _____

10. 45 ÷ 5 = _____

Division Facts

Test Items 1–15

Two Symbols for Division

Directions: Solve each division problem.

Division can be written several ways. The two most common forms are with

the division sign ÷ and the "division house" $\overline{)}$

$$12 ÷ 4 = 3$$

$$4\overline{)12}^3$$

Twelve divided by four is three.   Twelve divided by four is three.

1. 35 ÷ 5 = _____   2. $5\overline{)35}$

3. 48 ÷ 6 = _____   4. $6\overline{)48}$

5. 24 ÷ 6 = _____   6. $6\overline{)24}$

7. 81 ÷ 9 = _____   8. $9\overline{)81}$

9. 16 ÷ 2 = _____   10. $2\overline{)16}$

11. 32 ÷ 8 = _____   12. $8\overline{)32}$

CD-104225   •   Jump Into Math   •   © Carson-Dellosa

Skip Counting
Backward by 3s

Division Facts

Test Items 1–15

Directions: Use the hundreds chart below to help you skip count backward by 3s. Start at 99 and circle each multiple of 3. Color each circled number yellow.

100	99	98	97	96	95	94	93	92	91
90	89	88	87	86	85	84	83	82	81
80	79	78	77	76	75	74	73	72	71
70	69	68	67	66	65	64	63	62	61
60	59	58	57	56	55	54	53	52	51
50	49	48	47	46	45	44	43	42	41
40	39	38	37	36	35	34	33	32	31
30	29	28	27	26	25	24	23	22	21
20	19	18	17	16	15	14	13	12	11
10	9	8	7	6	5	4	3	2	1

Find the quotient for each division fact.

1. $27 \div 3 =$ _____

2. $12 \div 3 =$ _____

3. $15 \div 3 =$ _____

4. $9 \div 3 =$ _____

5. $6 \div 3 =$ _____

6. $21 \div 3 =$ _____

7. $3 \div 3 =$ _____

8. $18 \div 3 =$ _____

9. $24 \div 3 =$ _____

10. $0 \div 3 =$ _____

NAME: _____ DATE: _____

Skip Counting Backward by 4s

Directions: Use the hundred chart below to help you skip count backward by 4s. Start at 100 and circle each multiple of 4. Color each circled number orange.

100	99	98	97	96	95	94	93	92	91
90	89	88	87	86	85	84	83	82	81
80	79	78	77	76	75	74	73	72	71
70	69	68	67	66	65	64	63	62	61
60	59	58	57	56	55	54	53	52	51
50	49	48	47	46	45	44	43	42	41
40	39	38	37	36	35	34	33	32	31
30	29	28	27	26	25	24	23	22	21
20	19	18	17	16	15	14	13	12	11
10	9	8	7	6	5	4	3	2	1

Find the quotient for each division fact.

1. 28 ÷ 4 = _____

2. 12 ÷ 4 = _____

3. 24 ÷ 4 = _____

4. 8 ÷ 4 = _____

5. 4 ÷ 4 = _____

6. 32 ÷ 4 = _____

7. 0 ÷ 4 = _____

8. 20 ÷ 4 = _____

9. 36 ÷ 4 = _____

10. 16 ÷ 4 = _____

CD-104225 • Jump Into Math • © Carson-Dellosa

Number Line
Division by 3s

Division Facts

Test Items 1–15

Directions: Use the number lines to help you count backward by 3s.

Example: Start at 12. Count backward by 3s. Write the division fact.

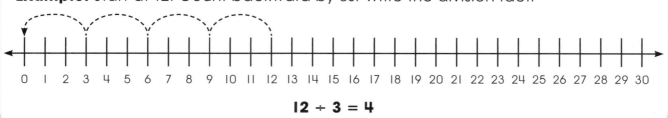

$$12 \div 3 = 4$$

1. Start at 24. Count backward by 3s. Write the division fact.

_____

2. Start at 27. Count backward by 3s. Write the division fact.

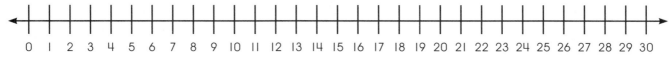

_____

3. Start at 9. Count backward by 3s. Write the division fact.

_____

4. Start at 21. Count backward by 3s. Write the division fact.

_____

Number Line Division by 4s

Directions: Use the number lines to help you count backward by 4s.

Example: Start at 12. Count backward by 4s. Write the division fact.

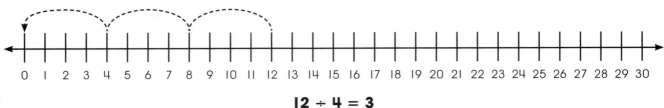

$$12 \div 4 = 3$$

1. Start at 24. Count backward by 4s. Write the division fact.

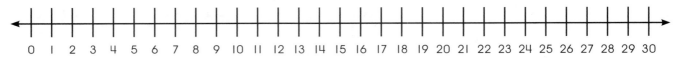

_____

2. Start at 28. Count backward by 4s. Write the division fact.

_____

3. Start at 16. Count backward by 4s. Write the division fact.

_____

4. Start at 20. Count backward by 4s. Write the division fact.

_____

   CD-104225 • Jump Into Math • © Carson-Dellosa

6s and 7s: Putting the Facts Together

Division Facts

Test Items 1–15

Directions: Write two division facts for each set of numbers.

1. 42, 6, 7

    _____
    _____

2. 2, 7, 14

    _____
    _____

3. 6, 18, 3

    _____
    _____

4. 56, 8, 7

    _____
    _____

5. 5, 7, 35

    _____
    _____

6. 54, 6, 9

    _____
    _____

7. 8, 48, 6

    _____
    _____

8. 8, 7, 56

    _____
    _____

9. 6, 30, 5

    _____
    _____

10. 4, 6, 24

    _____
    _____

11. 3, 21, 7

    _____
    _____

12. 9, 63, 7

    _____
    _____

Division Facts

Test Items 1–15

6s and 7s:
Numbers in a Box

Directions: Divide the numbers in each box by the number given. Write the quotients on the lines below each box.

1.   Divide by 6.

> 18, 12, 30

___3___ , ___2___ , ___5___

2.   Divide by 7.

> 21, 35, 7

_____ , _____ , _____

3.   Divide by 6.

> 6, 36, 48

_____ , _____ , _____

4.   Divide by 7.

> 63, 7, 56

_____ , _____ , _____

5.   Divide by 6.

> 60, 30, 12

_____ , _____ , _____

6.   Divide by 7.

> 42, 21, 49

_____ , _____ , _____

7.   Divide by 6.

> 54, 42, 6

_____ , _____ , _____

8.   Divide by 7.

> 14, 35, 70

_____ , _____ , _____

9.   Divide by 6.

> 60, 18, 30

_____ , _____ , _____

10.   Divide by 7.

> 21, 63, 28

_____ , _____ , _____

CD-104225 • Jump Into Math • © Carson-Dellosa

8s and 9s: Putting the Facts Together

Division Facts

Test Items 1–15

Directions: Write two division facts for each set of numbers.

1. 8, 40, 5

   _____

   _____

2. 6, 9, 54

   _____

   _____

3. 8, 56, 7

   _____

   _____

4. 5, 45, 9

   _____

   _____

5. 6, 8, 48

   _____

   _____

6. 3, 27, 9

   _____

   _____

7. 4, 36, 9

   _____

   _____

8. 8, 32, 4

   _____

   _____

9. 8, 9, 72

   _____

   _____

10. 3, 24, 8

   _____

   _____

11. 8, 2, 16

   _____

   _____

12. 10, 8, 80

   _____

   _____

Division Facts

Test Items 1–15

8s and 9s: Numbers in a Box

Directions: Divide the numbers in each box by the number given. Write the quotients on the lines below each box.

1. Divide by 8.

   | 24, 16, 48 |

   __3__ , __2__ , __6__

2. Divide by 9.

   | 45, 18, 9 |

   _____ , _____ , _____

3. Divide by 8.

   | 64, 32, 8 |

   _____ , _____ , _____

4. Divide by 9.

   | 54, 63, 27 |

   _____ , _____ , _____

5. Divide by 8.

   | 72, 56, 40 |

   _____ , _____ , _____

6. Divide by 9.

   | 45, 54, 81 |

   _____ , _____ , _____

7. Divide by 8.

   | 8, 16, 48 |

   _____ , _____ , _____

8. Divide by 9.

   | 72, 0, 36 |

   _____ , _____ , _____

9. Divide by 8.

   | 56, 72, 64 |

   _____ , _____ , _____

10. Divide by 9.

    | 81, 18, 9 |

    _____ , _____ , _____

Speed Drill:
1s, 2s, and 3s Facts

Division Facts

Test Items 1–15

Directions: Divide. Write your answer to each problem.

1. $18 \div 2 =$ _____

2. $0 \div 3 =$ _____

3. $9 \div 1 =$ _____

4. $15 \div 3 =$ _____

5. $10 \div 2 =$ _____

6. $3 \div 3 =$ _____

7. $16 \div 2 =$ _____

8. $10 \div 1 =$ _____

9. $6 \div 2 =$ _____

10. $21 \div 3 =$ _____

11. $4 \div 2 =$ _____

12. $9 \div 1 =$ _____

13. $2 \div 2 =$ _____

14. $18 \div 3 =$ _____

15. $3\overline{)3}$

16. $2\overline{)18}$

17. $1\overline{)10}$

18. $3\overline{)27}$

19. $2\overline{)12}$

20. $3\overline{)9}$

21. $1\overline{)5}$

22. $2\overline{)16}$

23. $3\overline{)24}$

24. $1\overline{)8}$

25. $3\overline{)15}$

26. $2\overline{)24}$

27. $3\overline{)18}$

28. $2\overline{)2}$

Division Facts

Test Items 1–15

Speed Drill:
4s, 5s, and 6s Facts

Directions: Divide. Write your answer to each problem.

1. $8 \div 4 =$ _____

2. $10 \div 5 =$ _____

3. $12 \div 6 =$ _____

4. $0 \div 4 =$ _____

5. $20 \div 5 =$ _____

6. $30 \div 6 =$ _____

7. $20 \div 4 =$ _____

8. $25 \div 5 =$ _____

9. $36 \div 6 =$ _____

10. $24 \div 4 =$ _____

11. $30 \div 5 =$ _____

12. $42 \div 6 =$ _____

13. $28 \div 4 =$ _____

14. $35 \div 5 =$ _____

15. $5\overline{)5}$

16. $6\overline{)0}$

17. $4\overline{)32}$

18. $5\overline{)40}$

19. $6\overline{)36}$

20. $4\overline{)24}$

21. $5\overline{)25}$

22. $6\overline{)36}$

23. $4\overline{)16}$

24. $5\overline{)10}$

25. $6\overline{)48}$

26. $4\overline{)8}$

27. $5\overline{)5}$

28. $6\overline{)54}$

CD-104225 • Jump Into Math • © Carson-Dellosa

Speed Drill: 7s, 8s, and 9s Facts

Division Facts

Test Items 1–15

Directions: Divide. Write your answer to each problem.

1. $45 \div 9 =$ _____

2. $8 \div 8 =$ _____

3. $63 \div 7 =$ _____

4. $0 \div 9 =$ _____

5. $48 \div 8 =$ _____

6. $14 \div 7 =$ _____

7. $54 \div 9 =$ _____

8. $49 \div 7 =$ _____

9. $16 \div 8 =$ _____

10. $18 \div 9 =$ _____

11. $21 \div 7 =$ _____

12. $56 \div 8 =$ _____

13. $63 \div 9 =$ _____

14. $28 \div 7 =$ _____

15. $7 \overline{)0}$

16. $8 \overline{)72}$

17. $9 \overline{)27}$

18. $7 \overline{)14}$

19. $8 \overline{)40}$

20. $9 \overline{)81}$

21. $7 \overline{)49}$

22. $8 \overline{)64}$

23. $7 \overline{)35}$

24. $9 \overline{)36}$

25. $8 \overline{)56}$

26. $7 \overline{)7}$

27. $9 \overline{)72}$

28. $8 \overline{)64}$

Speed Drill: Mixed Practice 1

Directions: Divide. Write your answer to each problem.

1. $32 \div 4 =$ _____

2. $35 \div 5 =$ _____

3. $14 \div 7 =$ _____

4. $18 \div 3 =$ _____

5. $30 \div 6 =$ _____

6. $24 \div 8 =$ _____

7. $81 \div 9 =$ _____

8. $28 \div 4 =$ _____

9. $6 \div 3 =$ _____

10. $32 \div 8 =$ _____

11. $35 \div 5 =$ _____

12. $54 \div 6 =$ _____

13. $30 \div 5 =$ _____

14. $6 \div 2 =$ _____

15. $9 \div 3 =$ _____

16. $42 \div 7 =$ _____

17. $18 \div 2 =$ _____

18. $40 \div 8 =$ _____

19. $12 \div 2 =$ _____

20. $12 \div 3 =$ _____

21. $18 \div 9 =$ _____

22. $56 \div 7 =$ _____

23. $14 \div 2 =$ _____

24. $20 \div 4 =$ _____

25. $16 \div 8 =$ _____

26. $48 \div 6 =$ _____

27. $24 \div 3 =$ _____

28. $15 \div 5 =$ _____

CD-104225 • Jump Into Math • © Carson-Dellosa

Speed Drill: Mixed Practice 2

Division Facts

Test Items 1–15

Directions: Divide. Write your answer to each problem.

1. $16 \div 8 =$ _____

2. $48 \div 8 =$ _____

3. $16 \div 2 =$ _____

4. $7 \div 1 =$ _____

5. $42 \div 6 =$ _____

6. $14 \div 2 =$ _____

7. $48 \div 6 =$ _____

8. $24 \div 6 =$ _____

9. $12 \div 4 =$ _____

10. $54 \div 9 =$ _____

11. $72 \div 9 =$ _____

12. $7 \div 7 =$ _____

13. $24 \div 3 =$ _____

14. $36 \div 4 =$ _____

15. $63 \div 7 =$ _____

16. $9 \div 1 =$ _____

17. $8 \div 2 =$ _____

18. $20 \div 4 =$ _____

19. $15 \div 5 =$ _____

20. $5 \div 1 =$ _____

21. $8 \div 4 =$ _____

22. $27 \div 9 =$ _____

23. $18 \div 3 =$ _____

24. $25 \div 5 =$ _____

25. $72 \div 8 =$ _____

26. $56 \div 7 =$ _____

27. $72 \div 9 =$ _____

28. $36 \div 9 =$ _____

Speed Drill: Mixed Practice 3

Directions: Divide. Write your answer to each problem.

1. $1\overline{)2}$	8. $4\overline{)32}$	15. $2\overline{)2}$	22. $9\overline{)18}$
2. $6\overline{)36}$	9. $2\overline{)20}$	16. $6\overline{)24}$	23. $2\overline{)16}$
3. $8\overline{)40}$	10. $4\overline{)24}$	17. $5\overline{)20}$	24. $9\overline{)27}$
4. $7\overline{)28}$	11. $8\overline{)72}$	18. $7\overline{)42}$	25. $5\overline{)10}$
5. $9\overline{)63}$	12. $6\overline{)12}$	19. $3\overline{)21}$	26. $8\overline{)16}$
6. $5\overline{)45}$	13. $3\overline{)24}$	20. $4\overline{)12}$	27. $8\overline{)56}$
7. $2\overline{)6}$	14. $8\overline{)72}$	21. $5\overline{)25}$	28. $3\overline{)27}$

Speed Drill: Mixed Practice 4

Division Facts

Test Items 1–15

Directions: Divide. Write your answer to each problem.

1. $2\overline{)4}$

2. $4\overline{)36}$

3. $7\overline{)35}$

4. $5\overline{)30}$

5. $3\overline{)12}$

6. $6\overline{)18}$

7. $9\overline{)9}$

8. $8\overline{)64}$

9. $7\overline{)42}$

10. $9\overline{)63}$

11. $8\overline{)32}$

12. $5\overline{)25}$

13. $3\overline{)24}$

14. $5\overline{)40}$

15. $8\overline{)56}$

16. $3\overline{)27}$

17. $2\overline{)10}$

18. $9\overline{)27}$

19. $7\overline{)28}$

20. $6\overline{)12}$

21. $9\overline{)18}$

22. $8\overline{)24}$

23. $2\overline{)16}$

24. $5\overline{)35}$

25. $6\overline{)30}$

26. $4\overline{)20}$

27. $8\overline{)32}$

28. $3\overline{)27}$

Division Facts

Test Items 1–15

Speed Drill: Missing Parts

Directions: Find the missing numbers.

1. $6 \div 3 =$ _____

2. $16 \div$ _____ $= 8$

3. _____ $\div 4 = 4$

4. $6 \div$ _____ $= 1$

5. _____ $\div 8 = 3$

6. $45 \div 5 =$ _____

7. _____ $\div 1 = 5$

8. $49 \div 7 =$ _____

9. $54 \div$ _____ $= 6$

10. _____ $\div 3 = 9$

11. $18 \div$ _____ $= 3$

12. $72 \div 9 =$ _____

13. $48 \div$ _____ $= 6$

14. _____ $\div 5 = 5$

15. $14 \div 7 =$ _____

16. _____ $\div 2 = 9$

17. $28 \div$ _____ $= 7$

18. $4 \div 1 =$ _____

19. $24 \div$ _____ $= 3$

20. $10 \div 2 =$ _____

21. $9 \div$ _____ $= 1$

22. _____ $\div 7 = 8$

23. _____ $\div 5 = 9$

24. _____ $\div 3 = 2$

25. _____ $\div 4 = 6$

26. $42 \div$ _____ $= 7$

27. $32 \div$ _____ $= 4$

28. $20 \div 4 =$ _____

CD-104225 • Jump Into Math • © Carson-Dellosa

Diagnostic Test:
Expanding on Multiplication and Division

Directions: Write your answer to each question in the space provided.

Part I: Multiplication

1. Write a multiplication sentence for the model below.

    _____ x _____ = 44

2. Write a multiplication sentence for the model below.

    _____ x _____ = 48

3. Write a multiplication sentence for the model below.

    _____ x _____ = 105

4. Write a multiplication sentence for the model below.

    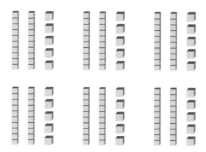

    _____ x _____ = _____

5. Write a multiplication sentence for the model below.

    _____ x _____ = _____

6. Multiply.

$$\begin{array}{r} 24 \\ \times\ 6 \\ \hline \end{array}$$

7. Multiply.

$$\begin{array}{r} 14 \\ \times\ 3 \\ \hline \end{array}$$

8. Multiply.

$$\begin{array}{r} 16 \\ \times\ 5 \\ \hline \end{array}$$

9. Multiply.

$$\begin{array}{r} 363 \\ \times\ 4 \\ \hline \end{array}$$

10. Multiply.

$$\begin{array}{r} 234 \\ \times\ 9 \\ \hline \end{array}$$

TEACHER ASSESSMENT AREA

Directions: Shade the boxes that correspond to correct test items.

TOTAL CORRECT: _____

Skill	Item Number				
Multiplication Models	1	2	3	4	5
Multiplying Two- and Three-Digit Numbers by One-Digit Numbers	6	7	8	9	10

Teacher Notes and Activities

TEACHER NOTES: Multiplication Models

(Diagnostic Test Part I: Test Items 1–5)

When students are comfortable with the memorization of the basic multiplication facts, introduce two-digit by one-digit multiplication. Use the 11s and 12s facts to model the multiplication algorithm. Some textbooks include the 11s and 12s facts as part of the basic multiplication facts table, stressing memorization rather than an understanding of the process. Spend time modeling the multiplication algorithm using the 11s and 12s facts because students already know the 1s, 2s, and 10s facts. Students can use their knowledge of these facts to learn the 11s and 12s facts, as shown in the methods below.

TEACHING ACTIVITIES

"How Many Ones and Tens?" (Multiplication Models)

Many students can quickly learn the 11s facts because of their knowledge of place value and their mastery of other multiplication facts. The 11s facts should be the first time students multiply a two-digit number by a one-digit number, except for the 10s. Use this model as an introduction to multiplying larger numbers.

---

3 x 11
(3 x 10) + (3 x 1)

Step 1: Regroup the 11 into 1 ten and 1 one.
Multiply the ten and one by 3.

Step 2: Add the products: 3 x 1 = 3 and 3 x 10 = 30.

Step 3: Write the number sentence: 3 x 11 = 33.

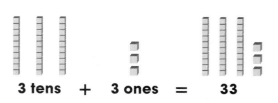

3 tens   +   3 ones   =   33

Try an example like the one below for the 12s facts.

6 x 12
(6 x 10) + (6 x 2)

6 tens   +   6 groups of 2 ones

Regroup 12 ones into 1 ten, 2 ones

7 tens   +   2 ones   =   72

Provide each student with a set of base ten blocks. Instruct students to model the following problems:
5 x 11 and **4 x 12.**

"Partial Product Method" (Multiplication Models)

When students have had plenty of practice modeling problems, introduce the partial product method as shown below. Allow students to use models as they work until they are comfortable with the algorithm.

9 x 11

Step 1: Multiply the ones.
Write the product as shown.
Step 2: Multiply the tens.
Write the product as shown.
Step 3: Add the partial products.

$$\begin{array}{r} 11 \\ \times\ 9 \\ \hline 9 \\ +\ 90 \\ \hline 99 \end{array}$$

  9   (9 x 1)
+ 90 (9 x 10)
 99   (Add.)

9 x 11 = 99

8 x 12

Step 1: Multiply the ones.
Write the product as shown.
Step 2: Multiply the tens.
Write the product as shown.
Step 3: Add the partial products.

$$\begin{array}{r} 12 \\ \times\ 8 \\ \hline 16 \\ +\ 80 \\ \hline 96 \end{array}$$

 16   (8 x 2)
+ 80 (8 x 10)
 96   (Add.)

8 x 12 = 96

CD-104225 • Jump Into Math • © Carson-Dellosa

"Chart the Products" (Multiplication Models)

Provide students with copies of both 11s charts and 12s charts. Instruct students to work each problem on notebook paper using the partial product method. Then, students should write the products into the charts.

Multiply by 11	**Multiply by 12**
11 x 1 = _____	12 x 1 = _____
11 x 2 = _____	12 x 2 = _____
11 x 3 = _____	12 x 3 = _____
11 x 4 = _____	12 x 4 = _____
11 x 5 = _____	12 x 5 = _____
11 x 6 = _____	12 x 6 = _____
11 x 7 = _____	12 x 7 = _____
11 x 8 = _____	12 x 8 = _____
11 x 9 = _____	12 x 9 = _____

TEACHER NOTES:

Multiplying Two- and Three-Digit Numbers by One-Digit Numbers
(Diagnostic Test Part I: Test Items 6–10)

After developmental work with 11s and 12s, students should be prepared to multiply larger two- and three-digit numbers. Continue teaching the partial product method with larger numbers. Stress the importance of place value in how the partial products are written underneath each problem. Model several problems using base ten blocks before introducing the formal algorithm. You may wish to use a place value chart when introducing problems with the formal algorithm. This will help students to see the relationship between place value and multiplication.

TEACHING DEMONSTRATION
(Multiplying Two- and Three-Digit Numbers by One-Digit Numbers)

Using a chalkboard or an overhead projector, model several problems that require multiplication of larger numbers. Use the following problem as an example.

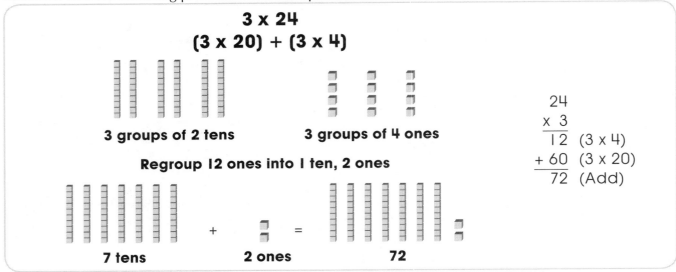

3 x 24

(3 x 20) + (3 x 4)

3 groups of 2 tens   3 groups of 4 ones

Regroup 12 ones into 1 ten, 2 ones

7 tens   +   2 ones   =   72

$$\begin{array}{r} 24 \\ \times\ 3 \\ \hline 12 \ (3 \times 4) \\ +\ 60 \ (3 \times 20) \\ \hline 72 \ (\text{Add}) \end{array}$$

TEACHING ACTIVITIES
"You Can Make Models Too!"
(Multiplying Two- and Three-Digit Numbers by One-Digit Numbers)

Show students how they can make their own models of multiplication problems. Instead of using base ten blocks, students should use tally marks (| | |) to represent tens and dots (•••) to represent ones. Prepare a blank worksheet chart similar to the following chart. Instruct students to make models of each problem, then solve the problems using the partial product method.

PROBLEM	MODEL	PARTIAL PRODUCT METHOD
1. $\begin{array}{r} 26 \\ \times\ 3 \end{array}$	‖ ‖ ‖ + (18 dots) Regroup 18 ones into 1 ten, 8 ones ‖ ‖ ‖ | + ••••••••	$\begin{array}{r} 26 \\ \times\ 3 \\ \hline 18\ (3 \times 6) \\ +\ 60\ (3 \times 20) \\ \hline 78\ (\text{Add.}) \end{array}$
2. $\begin{array}{r} 35 \\ \times\ 4 \end{array}$	‖‖ ‖‖ ‖‖ ‖‖ + (20 dots) Regroup 20 ones into 2 tens ‖‖ ‖‖ ‖‖ ‖‖ ‖‖	$\begin{array}{r} 35 \\ \times\ 4 \\ \hline 20\ (4 \times 5) \\ +\ 120\ (4 \times 30) \\ \hline 140\ (\text{Add.}) \end{array}$

CD-104225 • Jump Into Math • © Carson-Dellosa

PROBLEM	MODEL	PARTIAL PRODUCT METHOD
3. 43 x 8		
4. 56 x 5		
5. 28 x 4		
6. 33 x 5		
7. 42 x 8		
8. 68 x 2		
9. 73 x 4		
10. 88 x 2		

"Pulling Multiplication Together"
(Multiplying Two- and Three-Digit Numbers by One-Digit Numbers)

To help students learn the formal multiplication algorithm, begin by presenting problems in place value charts. This will help students to see the relationship between the partial products method and the formal algorithm.

Example 1:

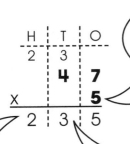

Step 1: Multiply the ones: 5 x 7 = 35. Write the 5 in the ones column. Regroup the 30 ones into 3 tens. Write 3 above the tens column.

Step 2: Multiply the tens: 5 x 4 = 20. Add the 3 tens: 20 tens + 3 tens = 23 tens. Write the 3 under the tens column. Regroup the 20 tens into 2 hundreds. Write the 2 above the hundreds column.

Step 3: There are no hundreds to multiply, so bring down the 2 hundreds. Write 2 under the hundreds column.

Example 2:

Step 1: Multiply the ones: 4 x 6 = 24. Write the 4 under the ones column. Regroup the 20 ones into 2 tens. Write the 2 above the tens column.

Step 2: Multiply the tens: 4 x 5 = 20. Add the 2 tens: 20 tens + 2 tens = 22 tens. Write the 2 under the tens column. Regroup the 20 tens into 2 hundreds. Write the 2 above the hundreds column.

Step 3: Multiply the hundreds: 4 x 3 = 12. Add the 2 hundreds: 12 hundreds + 2 hundreds = 14 hundreds. Write the 4 under the hundreds column. Regroup the 10 hundreds into 1 thousand. Write the 1 above the thousands column.

Step 4: There are no thousands to multiply, so bring down the 1 thousand. Write 1 under the thousands column.

Translating Models

Multiplication Models

Test Items 1–5

Directions: Write a number sentence to describe each model.

1.

_____ X _____ = _____
(Number   (Number in
of groups)   each group)

2.

_____ X _____ = _____

3.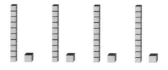

_____ X _____ = _____

4.

_____ X _____ = _____

5.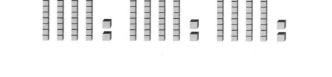

_____ X _____ = _____

6.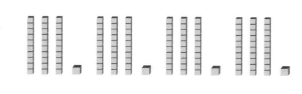

_____ X _____ = _____

7.

_____ X _____ = _____

8.

_____ X _____ = _____

Translating More Models

Multiplication Models

Test Items 1–5

Directions: Write a number sentence to describe each model.

1.

_____ X _____ = _____
(Number   (Number in
of groups)   each group)

2.

_____ X _____ = _____

3.

_____ X _____ = _____

4.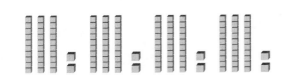

_____ X _____ = _____

5.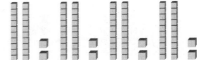

_____ X _____ = _____

6.

_____ X _____ = _____

7.

_____ X _____ = _____

8.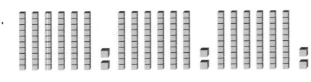

_____ X _____ = _____

 CD-104225 • Jump Into Math • © Carson-Dellosa

NAME: _____ DATE: _____

Even More Models

Directions: Write a number sentence to describe each model.

1.

_____ X _____ = _____
(Number of groups)   (Number in each group)

2.

_____ X _____ = _____

3.

_____ X _____ = _____

4.

_____ X _____ = _____

5.

_____ X _____ = _____

6.

_____ X _____ = _____

7.

_____ X _____ = _____

8.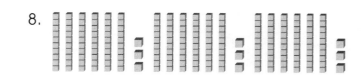

_____ X _____ = _____

Make Your Own Models

Directions: Follow the example to model each problem. Then, write each product in standard and expanded form.

Example: Make a model of each multiplication problem.
Use tally marks (||||) to represent tens and dots (•••) to represent ones.

PROBLEM	EXPANDED FORM	MODEL
45 x 3 — 135	(3 x 40) + (3 x 5)	• • • • • |||| |||| |||| + • • • • • • • • • • Regroup: |||| |||| |||| | + • • • • • Add: 13 tens + 5 ones = 135

PROBLEM	EXPANDED FORM	MODEL
1. 23 x 2	(___ x ___) + (___ x ___)	Regroup: Add:
2. 34 x 4	(___ x ___) + (___ x ___)	Regroup: Add:
3. 21 x 3	(___ x ___) + (___ x ___)	Regroup: Add:
4. 19 x 3	(___ X ___) + (___ x ___)	Regroup: Add:

Make Your Own Models

Directions: Follow the example to model each problem. Then, write each product in standard and expanded form.

Example: Make a model of each multiplication problem.
Use tally marks (||||) to represent tens and dots (•••) to represent ones.

PROBLEM	EXPANDED FORM	MODEL
53 x 4 212	(4 x 50) + (4 x 3)	||||| ||||| ||||| ||||| + ••• ••• ••• ••• Regroup: ||||| ||||| ||||| |||||	+ •• Add: 21 tens + 2 ones = 212

PROBLEM	EXPANDED FORM	MODEL
1. 18 x 2	(___ x ___) + (___ x ___)	Regroup: Add:
2. 44 x 3	(___ x ___) + (___ x ___)	Regroup: Add:
3. 22 x 4	(___ x ___) + (___ x ___)	Regroup: Add:
4. 29 x 2	(___ X ___) + (___ x ___)	Regroup: Add:

Multiplication Models
Test Items 1–5

Partial Product Method

Directions: Follow the example to model each problem. Then, use the partial product method to find each product.

Example: Use tally marks (|||) to represent tens and dots (•••) to represent ones.

PROBLEM	MODEL	PARTIAL PRODUCT
26 x 2 52	|| || + •••••• •••••• Regroup: || || | + •• Add: 5 tens + 2 ones = 52	26 x 2 12 (2 x 6) + 40 (2 x 20) 52

PROBLEM	MODEL	PARTIAL PRODUCT
1. 25 x 4	Regroup: Add:	
2. 41 x 5	Regroup: Add:	
3. 32 x 6	Regroup: Add:	

CD-104225 • Jump Into Math • © Carson-Dellosa

Multiplication Charts

Directions: Multiply. Regroup when needed.

1.

H	T	O
	2	7
x		6

2.

H	T	O
	3	5
x		4

3.

H	T	O
	4	3
x		4

4.

H	T	O
	5	6
x		5

5.

H	T	O
	5	2
x		4

6.

H	T	O
	6	4
x		3

7.

H	T	O
	7	2
x		3

8.

H	T	O
	6	2
x		9

9.

H	T	O
	8	2
x		2

10.

H	T	O
	9	1
x		3

11.

H	T	O
	4	7
x		5

12.

H	T	O
	7	4
x		5

Multiplying Two- and
Three-Digit Numbers by
One-Digit Numbers

Test Items 6–10

Multiplying in Place

Directions: Multiply. Regroup when needed.

1.

H	T	O
	1	4
x		6

2.

H	T	O
	2	8
x		7

3.

H	T	O
	5	6
x		6

4.

H	T	O
	9	4
x		8

5.

H	T	O
	5	4
x		4

6.

H	T	O
	6	4
x		8

7.

H	T	O
	7	1
x		5

8.

H	T	O
	7	4
x		3

9.

H	T	O
	5	1
x		5

10.

H	T	O
	4	1
x		6

11.

H	T	O
	5	0
x		4

12.

H	T	O
	9	7
x		5

Multiplication Practice

Directions: Multiply. Regroup when needed.

1.

H	T	O
	8	9
x		9

5.

H	T	O
	7	6
x		8

9.

H	T	O
	4	8
x		7

13.

H	T	O
	9	8
x		6

2.

H	T	O
	2	3
x		7

6.

H	T	O
	2	4
x		6

10.

H	T	O
	5	2
x		9

14.

H	T	O
	6	4
x		9

3.

H	T	O
	7	0
x		6

7.

H	T	O
	1	8
x		5

11.

H	T	O
	5	3
x		5

15.

H	T	O
	3	7
x		3

4.

H	T	O
	4	9
x		4

8.

H	T	O
	5	9
x		5

12.

H	T	O
	7	7
x		5

16.

H	T	O
	7	2
x		5

Multiplying Two- and Three-Digit Numbers by One-Digit Numbers

Test Items 6–10

Multiplication Practice 2

Directions: Multiply. Regroup when needed.

1.
```
  H   T   O
      5   2
x         6
```

2.
```
  H   T   O
      3   6
x         7
```

3.
```
  H   T   O
      7   9
x         2
```

4.
```
  H   T   O
      8   6
x         5
```

5.
```
  H   T   O
      7   9
x         3
```

6.
```
  H   T   O
      8   4
x         5
```

7.
```
  H   T   O
      7   2
x         8
```

8.
```
  H   T   O
      6   3
x         6
```

9.
```
  H   T   O
      9   5
x         8
```

10.
```
  H   T   O
      4   7
x         9
```

11.
```
  H   T   O
      3   8
x         3
```

12.
```
  H   T   O
      4   8
x         4
```

13.
```
  H   T   O
      8   8
x         7
```

14.
```
  H   T   O
      5   5
x         8
```

15.
```
  H   T   O
      2   8
x         4
```

16.
```
  H   T   O
      8   1
x         6
```

     CD-104225 • Jump Into Math • © Carson-Dellosa

Pulling Multiplication Together

Multiplying Two- and Three-Digit Numbers by One-Digit Numbers

Test Items 6–10

Directions: Multiply. Regroup when needed.

1.   19
    x 4

2.   47
    x 5

3.   43
    x 3

4.   59
    x 7

5.   62
    x 9

6.   43
    x 8

7.   32
    x 4

8.   50
    x 6

9.   34
    x 5

10.   41
     x 4

11.   72
     x 6

12.   52
     x 7

13.   85
     x 4

14.   35
     x 5

15.   87
     x 4

Pulling Multiplication Together 2

Directions: Multiply. Regroup when needed.

1.   67
   x 5

2.   21
   x 8

3.   92
   x 9

4.   34
   x 7

5.   45
   x 9

6.   45
   x 8

7.   38
   x 7

8.   67
   x 6

9.   22
   x 9

10.   82
   x 2

11.   98
   x 6

12.   64
   x 9

13.   37
   x 3

14.   47
   x 6

15.   57
   x 5

Pulling Multiplication Together 3

Multiplying Two- and Three-Digit Numbers by One-Digit Numbers

Test Items 6–10

Directions: Multiply each problem. Regroup when needed.

1.   19
      x 5

2.   72
      x 6

3.   93
      x 4

4.   52
      x 6

5.   36
      x 7

6.   79
      x 8

7.   63
      x 9

8.   86
      x 5

9.   79
      x 3

10.   84
      x 6

11.   87
      x 4

12.   72
      x 9

13.   70
      x 5

14.   63
      x 6

15.   67
      x 7

Multiplying Two- and Three-Digit Numbers by One-Digit Numbers

Test Items 6–10

Multiplying Three-Digit Numbers

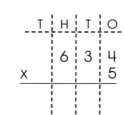

Directions: Multiply. Regroup when needed.

1.
T	H	T	O
	6	1	1
x			5

2.
T	H	T	O
	4	4	3
x			8

3.
T	H	T	O
	1	3	2
x			4

4.
T	H	T	O
	8	5	0
x			6

5.
T	H	T	O
	6	3	4
x			5

6.
T	H	T	O
	8	7	2
x			4

7.
T	H	T	O
	2	5	2
x			7

8.
T	H	T	O
	8	0	5
x			7

9.
T	H	T	O
	1	3	5
x			3

10.
T	H	T	O
	6	8	7
x			4

11.
T	H	T	O
	7	6	7
x			5

12.
T	H	T	O
	2	1	2
x			8

13.
T	H	T	O
	8	3	5
x			3

14.
T	H	T	O
	6	7	5
x			4

15.
T	H	T	O
	1	4	5
x			9

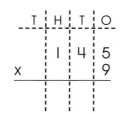

CD-104225 • Jump Into Math • © Carson-Dellosa

More Multiplying Three-Digit Numbers

Multiplying Two- and Three-Digit Numbers by One-Digit Numbers

Test Items 6–10

Directions: Multiply. Regroup when needed.

1.

T	H	T	O
	7	9	3
x			3

2.

T	H	T	O
	6	5	2
x			6

3.

T	H	T	O
	5	3	6
x			7

4.

T	H	T	O
	6	7	9
x			4

5.

T	H	T	O
	2	6	1
x			3

6.

T	H	T	O
	3	8	6
x			5

7.

T	H	T	O
	4	7	9
x			3

8.

T	H	T	O
	5	8	4
x			7

9.

T	H	T	O
	2	8	4
x			3

10.

T	H	T	O
	9	7	2
x			8

11.

T	H	T	O
	8	7	0
x			3

12.

T	H	T	O
	6	6	3
x			6

13.

T	H	T	O
	5	6	7
x			4

14.

T	H	T	O
	4	9	5
x			8

15.

T	H	T	O
	6	4	7
x			9

Multiplying Two- and
Three-Digit Numbers by
One-Digit Numbers

Test Items 6–10

Even More Multiplying Three-Digit Numbers

Directions: Multiply. Regroup when needed.

1.
T	H	T	O
	7	8	5
x			5

2.
T	H	T	O
	7	7	3
x			4

3.
T	H	T	O
	8	5	1
x			6

4.
T	H	T	O
	7	4	1
x			6

5.
T	H	T	O
	3	7	7
x			6

6.
T	H	T	O
	4	5	2
x			4

7.
T	H	T	O
	8	9	7
x			5

8.
T	H	T	O
	1	6	7
x			4

9.
T	H	T	O
	2	1	1
x			7

10.
T	H	T	O
	4	2	2
x			4

11.
T	H	T	O
	4	4	1
x			5

12.
T	H	T	O
	7	1	2
x			6

13.
T	H	T	O
	4	3	6
x			2

14.
T	H	T	O
	7	7	5
x			6

15.
T	H	T	O
	4	4	5
x			8

Pulling Multiplication Together 4

Multiplying Two- and Three-Digit Numbers by One-Digit Numbers

Test Items 6–10

Directions: Multiply. Regroup when needed.

1. 387
    x 5

2. 236
    x 6

3. 478
    x 4

4. 582
    x 5

5. 597
    x 3

6. 777
    x 4

7. 965
    x 9

8. 238
    x 8

9. 953
    x 7

10. 117
     x 7

11. 936
     x 5

12. 245
     x 6

13. 765
     x 2

14. 957
     x 4

15. 583
     x 6

Multiplying Two- and
Three-Digit Numbers by
One-Digit Numbers
Test Items 6–10

Pulling Multiplication Together 5

Directions: Multiply. Regroup when needed.

1.
$$\begin{array}{r} 419 \\ \times\ 4 \\ \hline \end{array}$$

2.
$$\begin{array}{r} 547 \\ \times\ 5 \\ \hline \end{array}$$

3.
$$\begin{array}{r} 643 \\ \times\ 3 \\ \hline \end{array}$$

4.
$$\begin{array}{r} 359 \\ \times\ 7 \\ \hline \end{array}$$

5.
$$\begin{array}{r} 262 \\ \times\ 9 \\ \hline \end{array}$$

6.
$$\begin{array}{r} 843 \\ \times\ 8 \\ \hline \end{array}$$

7.
$$\begin{array}{r} 932 \\ \times\ 4 \\ \hline \end{array}$$

8.
$$\begin{array}{r} 450 \\ \times\ 6 \\ \hline \end{array}$$

9.
$$\begin{array}{r} 634 \\ \times\ 5 \\ \hline \end{array}$$

10.
$$\begin{array}{r} 341 \\ \times\ 4 \\ \hline \end{array}$$

11.
$$\begin{array}{r} 772 \\ \times\ 6 \\ \hline \end{array}$$

12.
$$\begin{array}{r} 652 \\ \times\ 7 \\ \hline \end{array}$$

13.
$$\begin{array}{r} 785 \\ \times\ 4 \\ \hline \end{array}$$

14.
$$\begin{array}{r} 935 \\ \times\ 5 \\ \hline \end{array}$$

15.
$$\begin{array}{r} 487 \\ \times\ 4 \\ \hline \end{array}$$

CD-104225 • Jump Into Math • © Carson-Dellosa

Pulling Multiplication Together 6

Multiplying Two- and Three-Digit Numbers by One-Digit Numbers

Test Items 6–10

Directions: Multiply. Regroup when needed.

1. 219
   x 5

2. 472
   x 6

3. 693
   x 4

4. 852
   x 6

5. 136
   x 7

6. 379
   x 8

7. 563
   x 9

8. 786
   x 5

9. 979
   x 3

10. 284
    x 6

11. 487
    x 4

12. 672
    x 9

13. 770
    x 5

14. 563
    x 6

15. 367
    x 7

Diagnostic Test: Expanding on Multiplication and Division

Directions: Write your answer to each question in the space provided.

Part II: Division

1. Look at the pattern. Find the missing number.

$$4 \div 4 = 1$$
$$40 \div 4 = 10$$
$$400 \div 4 = \underline{\hspace{1cm}}$$

2. Look at the pattern. Find the missing number.

$$6 \div 6 = 1$$
$$60 \div 6 = \underline{\hspace{1cm}}$$
$$600 \div 6 = 100$$

3. Look at the pattern. Find the missing number.

$$3 \div 3 = 1$$
$$\underline{\hspace{1cm}} \div 3 = 10$$
$$300 \div 3 = 100$$

4. Jim has 24 books to put on 4 shelves. How many books go on each shelf?

_____ books on each shelf

5. Betsy has 36 pencils to divide among 6 friends. How many pencils does each friend get?

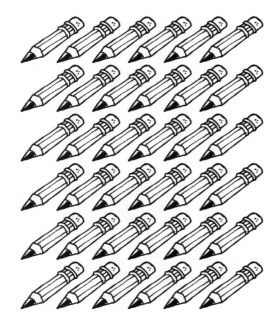

_____ pencils for each friend

6. 24 cupcakes in all.
   How many groups of 4? _____
   How many left over? _____

7. 24 turtles in all.
   How many groups of 5? _____
   How many left over? _____

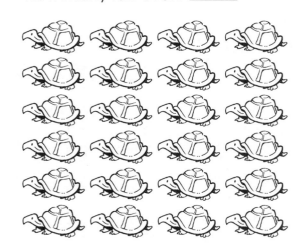

8. Find the largest number of 3s in 22.
   Then, find the remainder.

   22 = _____ groups of 3 + _____ left

9. Find the quotient and remainder.

   ____ R ____
   6)93

10. Find the quotient and remainder.

    ____ R ____
    5)54

TEACHER ASSESSMENT AREA

Directions: Shade the boxes that correspond to correct test items.

Skill	Item Number				
Division Patterns and Models	1	2	3	4	5
Division with Remainders	6	7	8	9	10

TOTAL CORRECT: _____

Teacher Notes and Activities

TEACHER NOTES: Division Patterns and Models
(Diagnostic Test Part II: Test Items 1–5)

To introduce the division algorithm, review the connection between multiplication and division. Some teachers rush into formal work with division before students develop a thorough understanding of prerequisite skills and concepts. The following teaching activities will help students understand the total concept of division in a step-by-step approach.

TEACHING ACTIVITIES

"Developing Division Skills and Concepts" (Division Patterns and Models)

Establish the relationship between multiplication and division. Demonstrate this concept by using pictorial arrays and the corresponding number sentences.

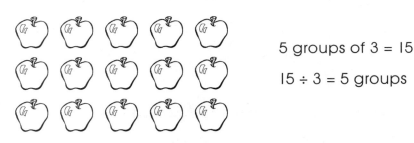

5 groups of 3 = 15

15 ÷ 3 = 5 groups

Ask students to write division sentences using the same numbers from multiplication sentences.

$$3 \times 6 = 18$$

$$\underline{\hspace{2cm}} \div \underline{\hspace{2cm}} = \underline{\hspace{2cm}}$$

Then, ask students to write multiplication and division sentences to describe pictorial arrays.

$$\underline{\hspace{2cm}} \times \underline{\hspace{2cm}} = \underline{\hspace{2cm}}$$

$$\underline{\hspace{2cm}} \div \underline{\hspace{2cm}} = \underline{\hspace{2cm}}$$

Give students a variety of pictorial arrays. Instruct them to practice writing multiplication and division sentences to describe the arrays.

"Multiplication and Division Patterns" (Division Patterns and Models)

1 x 1 = 1	1 ÷ 1 = 1
10 x 1 = 10	10 ÷ 1 = 10
100 x 1 = 100	100 ÷ 1 = 100
4 x 2 = 8	8 ÷ 4 = 2
40 x 2 = 80	80 ÷ 4 = 20
400 x 2 = 800	800 ÷ 4 = 200

Show students examples of related multiplication and division patterns like those above. Students should observe patterns and verbalize connections they can make between the multiplication and division problems. Then, instruct students to write the missing numbers to complete the multiplication and division patterns below.

3 x 3 = _____	9 ÷ _____ = 3
_____ x 3 = 90	90 ÷ 3 = 30
300 x _____ = 900	_____ ÷ 3 = 300

"Division Word Problems" (Division Patterns and Models)

Students need to be able to solve word problems. Division can be interpreted in two different ways, and students need to have experience with both: measurement (repeated subtraction) problems and partition (equal groups) problems.

Measurement (Repeated Subtraction) Division Problems

Jason has 20 CDs. His CD carrier holds 4 CDs on each page. How many pages will he need to hold all of his CDs?

$$4 \times \underline{\hspace{1cm}} = 20 \qquad 4\overline{)20}\,^{5}$$

Emily wants to cut ribbon to make bracelets. She has 24 inches of ribbon. How many 6-inch strips of ribbon can she make?

$$\underline{\hspace{1cm}} \times 6 = 24 \qquad 6\overline{)24}\,^{4}$$

Partition (Equal Groups) Division Problems

Janelle has 27 books and 3 shelves. How many books should she put on each shelf so that each shelf has an equal number of books?

$$27 = \underline{\hspace{1cm}} \times 3 \qquad 3\overline{)27}\,^{9}$$

Mr. Smith's classroom has 25 desks. How many desks could be placed in each row if Mr. Smith wants five equal rows?

$$25 = \underline{\hspace{1cm}} \times 5 \qquad 5\overline{)25}\,^{5}$$

TEACHER NOTES: Division with Remainders

(Diagnostic Test Part II: Test Items 6–10)

After students master the basic division facts, introduce division with remainders: finding the largest possible quotient and smallest remainder. Students should begin with models and pictorial representations.

TEACHING ACTIVITIES

"Finding a Quotient and Remainder" (Division with Remainders)

Give each student 24 counters. Ask students the following questions and instruct them to model their answers using the counters.

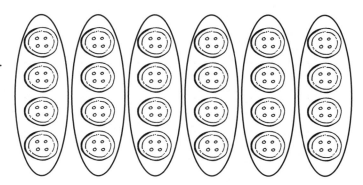

"How many groups of 4 can be made?"

Students should make 6 groups of 4 counters.

"How many are left over?"

Students should answer "0."

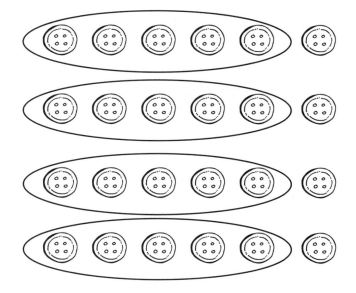

"How many groups of 5 can be made?"

Students should make 4 groups of 5 counters.

"How many are left over?"

Students should answer "4."

Continue this exercise with different numbers until students can answer correctly each time.

"Visual Models" (Division with Remainders)

Provide students with pictorial representations of sets of objects. Instruct students to divide the sets in different ways.

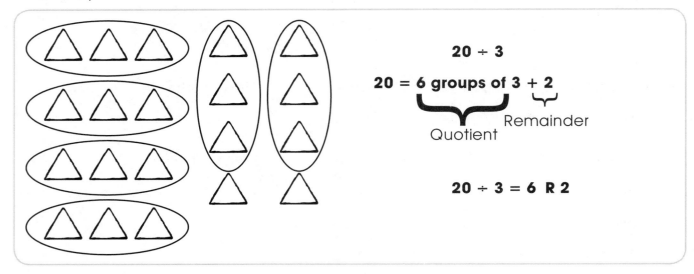

20 ÷ 3

20 = 6 groups of 3 + 2

Quotient   Remainder

20 ÷ 3 = 6 R 2

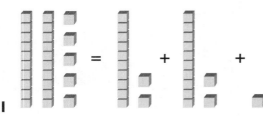

25 ÷ 2

Make two equal groups.
How many in each group? _____
How many left over? _____

25 ÷ 2 = 12 R 1

"Division without Remainders"

Students should begin working with models. Then, the formal division algorithm can be introduced.

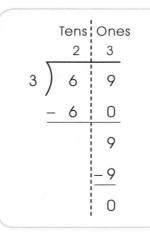

Step 1: Divide the tens.
6 tens ÷ 3 = 2 tens

Step 2: Multiply.
2 tens x 3 = 60

Step 3: Subtract.
69 – 60 = 9

Tens | Ones

Step 4: Divide the ones.
9 ones ÷ 3 = 3 ones

Step 5: Multiply.
3 ones x 3 = 9

Step 6: Subtract.
9 – 9 = 0 (no remainder)

"Division with Remainders"

Step 1: Divide the tens.
  6 tens ÷ 4 = 1 ten
  with 20 ones left over

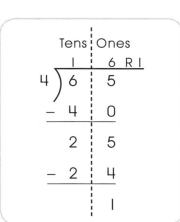

Step 4: Divide the ones.
  25 ones ÷ 4 = 6 ones
  with 1 one left over

Step 2: Multiply.
  1 ten x 4 = 40

Step 5: Multiply.
  6 ones x 4 = 24

Step 3: Subtract.
  65 – 40 = 25

Step 6: Subtract.
  25 – 24 = 1
  (1 is the remainder)

Have students practice the steps with the following problems.

1. $2\overline{)39}$ 2. $5\overline{)95}$ 3. $7\overline{)79}$

4. $4\overline{)60}$ 5. $5\overline{)27}$ 6. $3\overline{)93}$

7. $5\overline{)57}$ 8. $6\overline{)82}$ 9. $5\overline{)55}$

Division Patterns
and Models

Test Items 1–5

Write the Missing Numbers

Directions: Look at each pattern below. Write the missing numbers.

1. $3 \div 3 = 1$
     $30 \div 3 = 10$
     $300 \div 3 = $ _____

2. $6 \div 6 = 1$
     $60 \div 6 = 10$
     $600 \div 6 = $ _____

3. $8 \div 4 = 2$
     $80 \div 4 = $ _____
     $800 \div 4 = $ _____

4. $9 \div $ _____ $= 3$
     $90 \div 3 = 30$
     _____ $\div 3 = 300$

5. $4 \div 2 = 2$
     $40 \div 2 = $ _____
     _____ $\div 2 = $ _____

6. $10 \div 5 = 2$
     $100 \div 5 = $ _____
     $1,000 \div 5 = $ _____

7. $20 \div 10 = $ _____
     $200 \div 10 = $ _____
     $2,000 \div 100 = $ _____

8. $6 \div 2 = $ _____
     $60 \div 2 = $ _____
     _____ $\div 20 = 30$

9. $10 \div 2 = $ _____
     _____ $\div 20 = 5$
     $1,000 \div 200 = $ _____

10. $12 \div 4 = $ _____
     $120 \div 40 = $ _____
     $1,200 \div $ _____ $= 3$

How Many in Each Group?

Division Patterns and Models

Test Items 1–5

Directions: Look at each picture. Then, answer the questions and complete the division sentences.

1.

How many in all?

_____

How many equal groups?_____

How many in each group? _____

$12 \div 3 =$ _____

2.

How many in all?

_____

How many equal groups? _____

How many in each group? _____

$18 \div 3 =$ _____

3.

How many in all?

_____

How many equal groups? _____

How many in each group? _____

$15 \div 3 =$ _____

4.

$8 \div 2 =$ _____

5.

$9 \div 3 =$ _____

6.

$16 \div 4 =$ _____

7. Write a multiplication and division sentence to describe the picture.

_____ x _____ = _____

_____ ÷ _____ = _____

Division Patterns and Models

Test Items 1–5

Division Match

Directions: First, solve each division sentence. Then, write the letter of the matching picture before each division sentence.

_____ 1. 16 ÷ 8 = _____

_____ 2. 24 ÷ 4 = _____

_____ 3. 30 ÷ 5 = _____

_____ 4. 18 ÷ 6 = _____

_____ 5. 32 ÷ 4 = _____

_____ 6. 21 ÷ 3 = _____

A. △ △ △ △ △ △ △
△ △ △ △ △ △ △
△ △ △ △ △ △ △
△ △ △ △ △ △ △

B. ○ ○ ○ ○ ○
○ ○ ○ ○ ○
○ ○ ○ ○ ○
○ ○ ○ ○ ○
○ ○ ○ ○ ○

C. ♡ ♡ ♡ ♡ ♡ ♡
♡ ♡ ♡ ♡ ♡ ♡
♡ ♡ ♡ ♡ ♡ ♡

D. ☾ ☾ ☾ ☾ ☾ ☾ ☾ ☾ ☾
☾ ☾ ☾ ☾ ☾ ☾ ☾ ☾ ☾

E. ☆ ☆ ☆ ☆ ☆ ☆
☆ ☆ ☆ ☆ ☆ ☆
☆ ☆ ☆ ☆ ☆ ☆
☆ ☆ ☆ ☆ ☆ ☆

F. □ □ □ □ □ □
□ □ □ □ □ □
□ □ □ □ □ □

CD-104225 • Jump Into Math • © Carson-Dellosa

Word Problems with Division

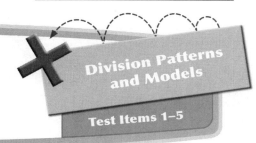

Division Patterns and Models

Test Items 1–5

Directions: Solve each division problem. Write the answer in the space provided.

1. Thomas has 27 books and 3 shelves. How many books should he put on each shelf so that each shelf has an equal number of books?

   _____

2. Charlie the Clown had 10 balls in his hat. He gave the same number of balls to each one of 10 children. How many balls did each child receive?

   _____

3. Diane bought 20 new CDs. Her CD carrier holds 4 CDs on each page. How many pages will she need to hold her new CDs?

   _____

4. There are 25 chips in a math game. If 5 students play the game, how many chips should each student get?

   _____

5. Charlotte wants to cut ribbon to make bracelets. She has 24 inches of ribbon. How many 6-inch strips of ribbon can she make?

   _____

6. Mr. Doran baked 75 chocolate chip cookies for the bake sale. If he puts 5 cookies in each package, how many packages will he need to sell?

   _____

7. Jessica bought 48 pencils. The pencils are wrapped in sets of 6. She wants to give them to her friends as gifts. How many sets can Jessica give as presents?

   _____

8. Ace Tire Company has 60 tires in its inventory. If each car that comes in needs 4 tires installed, how many cars can Ace Tire Company service?

   _____

Solving Problems with Division

Directions: Solve each division problem. Write the answer in the space provided.

1. Juan has 36 pencils to divide equally among 6 friends. How many pencils does each friend receive?

1. _____

2. April placed 32 dog bones into 4 boxes. How many dog bones are in each box?

2. _____

3. Lauren practices playing the piano for 30 minutes each day. She plays each piece she is assigned for 5 minutes. How many pieces of music does she practice each day?

3. _____

4. Three classes at Midvale Elementary collected a total of 84 aluminum cans together. Each class collected the same number of cans. How many cans did each class collect?

4. _____

5. Mrs. Moody's class sold 96 boxes of popcorn. If each student sold 8 boxes of popcorn, how many students are in Mrs. Moody's class?

5. _____

6. If Cesar splits a bag of 72 lollipops among 8 friends, how many lollipops will each friend receive?

6. _____

Division Fact Review

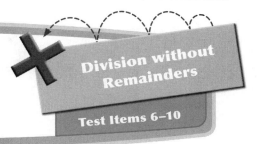

Division without Remainders

Test Items 6–10

Directions: Solve the following division problems.

1. $3\overline{)12}$

2. $4\overline{)20}$

3. $6\overline{)24}$

4. $7\overline{)35}$

5. $5\overline{)25}$

6. $5\overline{)35}$

7. $6\overline{)36}$

8. $7\overline{)49}$

9. $8\overline{)64}$

10. $8\overline{)72}$

11. $6\overline{)48}$

12. $7\overline{)42}$

13. $9\overline{)63}$

14. $9\overline{)72}$

15. $7\overline{)63}$

16. $9\overline{)81}$

Leftover Remainders

Directions: First, study the example below. Then, solve the division problems.

Example:	$\begin{array}{r}\mathbf{8\ R\ 3}\\4\overline{)35}\\-32\\\hline 3\end{array}$	**Think:** The closest multiple of 4 that is less than 35 is 32. 35 – 32 = **3**; so 3 is the **remainder**.

1. $2\overline{)47}$ 2. $3\overline{)52}$ 3. $4\overline{)65}$ 4. $5\overline{)24}$

5. $4\overline{)19}$ 6. $7\overline{)24}$ 7. $5\overline{)74}$ 8. $6\overline{)63}$

9. $8\overline{)67}$ 10. $7\overline{)87}$ 11. $6\overline{)37}$ 12. $7\overline{)51}$

13. $9\overline{)98}$ 14. $8\overline{)89}$ 15. $8\overline{)99}$ 16. $9\overline{)85}$

CD-104225 • Jump Into Math • © Carson-Dellosa

NAME: _____ DATE: _____

Remembering Remainders

Division with Remainders

Test Items 6–10

Directions: Solve the division problems. Do not forget the remainders.

1. $4\overline{)39}$ 2. $6\overline{)33}$ 3. $5\overline{)28}$ 4. $7\overline{)45}$

5. $5\overline{)27}$ 6. $7\overline{)48}$ 7. $8\overline{)60}$ 8. $5\overline{)81}$

9. $9\overline{)84}$ 10. $8\overline{)87}$ 11. $9\overline{)60}$ 12. $8\overline{)42}$

13. $7\overline{)78}$ 14. $8\overline{)35}$ 15. $7\overline{)88}$ 16. $8\overline{)98}$

Diagnostic Test:
Expanding on Multiplication and Division

Directions: Divide to find the quotient and remainder (if needed) for each problem.

Part III: Dividing Two- and Three-Digit Numbers by One-Digit Numbers

1. $5\overline{)73}$

2. $3\overline{)97}$

3. $7\overline{)81}$

4. $4\overline{)65}$

5. $6\overline{)58}$

6. $2\overline{)118}$

7.   8)369

9.   4)447

8.   9)888

10.   2)939

TEACHER ASSESSMENT AREA

Directions: Shade the boxes that correspond to correct test items.

TOTAL CORRECT: _____

Skill	Item Number				
Dividing Two-Digit Numbers by One-Digit Numbers	1	2	3	4	5
Dividing Three-Digit Numbers by One-Digit Numbers	6	7	8	9	10

Teacher Notes and Activities

TEACHER NOTES:
Dividing Two- and Three-Digit Numbers by One-Digit Numbers
(Diagnostic Test Part III: Test Items 1–10)

It is important to carefully develop each step in the division algorithm. Use place value charts to help students recognize hundreds, tens, and ones in division problems. Students should practice estimating quotients by studying tables of multiples. When students master division with place value charts, introduce the standard form of the division algorithm.

TEACHING ACTIVITIES

"Follow the Steps in Place" (Two- and Three-Digit by One-Digit Division)

Review the steps for division using place value charts. Demonstrate with the following problems. Then, instruct students to practice similar problems.

Two-Digit by One-Digit Division

Step 1: Divide the tens.

Step 2: Multiply.

Step 3: Subtract.

Step 4: Divide the ones.

Step 5: Multiply.

Step 6: Subtract.

Step 7: Find the remainder.

Example 1:

```
        Tens | Ones
           2 |  2   R 1
      3 )  6 |  7
        - 6 |  0   (20 x 3 = 60)
            |  7
        -   |  6   (2 x 3 = 6)
            |  1
```

Example 2:

```
        Tens | Ones
           2 |  1   R 3
      4 )  8 |  7
        - 8 |  0   (20 x 4 = 80)
            |  7
        -   |  4   (1 x 4 = 4)
            |  3
```

Three-Digit by One-Digit Division

Step 1: Divide the hundreds.

Step 2: Multiply.

Step 3: Subtract.

Step 4: Divide the tens.

Step 5: Multiply.

Step 6: Subtract.

Step 7: Divide the ones.

Step 8: Multiply.

Step 9: Subtract.

Step 10: Find the remainder.

Example 1:

```
      H : T : O
      2 : 1 : 4  R 1
   2 ) 4 : 2 : 9
     – 4 : 0 : 0   (200 x 2 = 400)
       : 2 : 9
       – 2 : 0   (10 x 2 = 20)
         : 9
         – 8   (4 x 2 = 8)
           : 1
```

Example 2:

```
      H : T : O
      3 : 1 : 6  R 1
   3 ) 9 : 4 : 9
     – 9 : 0 : 0   (300 x 3 = 900)
       : 4 : 9
       – 3 : 0   (10 x 3 = 30)
         : 1 : 9
         – 1 : 8   (6 x 3 = 18)
           : 1
```

Students should practice division problems by using place value charts and following the steps to divide both two- and three-digit numbers.

1.   3)73   2.   5)59   3.   4)97

4.   2)321   5.   5)763   6.   3)732

"Estimating the Quotient"
Dividing Two- and Three-Digit Numbers by One-Digit Numbers

References for multiples of divisors can help students estimate the quotient. This will help them to find starting places and make sure their answers are reasonable. This technique also serves as another way to emphasize the relationship between multiplication and division. Multiples provide support for students who may need extra help in mastering the difficult concept of division. A student can refer to multiples charts to see which multiple of a divisor is closest to a dividend without going over. Demonstrate with the following examples and monitor students' progress carefully.

Multiples of 6
10 x 6 = 60
20 x 6 = 120
30 x 6 = 180
40 x 6 = 240
50 x 6 = 300
60 x 6 = 360
70 x 6 = 420
80 x 6 = 480
90 x 6 = 540
100 x 6 = 600

Example 1:

```
      H | T | O
        | 2 | 2   R 3
  6 ) 1 | 3 | 5
    - 1 | 2 | 0   (20 x 6 = 120)
        | 1 | 5
      - | 1 | 2   (2 x 6 = 12)
        |   | 3
```

Example 2:

```
      H | T | O
        | 4 | 2   R 1
  6 ) 2 | 5 | 3
    - 2 | 4 | 0   (40 x 6 = 240)
        | 1 | 3
      - | 1 | 2   (2 x 6 = 12)
        |   | 1
```

Multiples of 5
10 x 5 = 50
20 x 5 = 100
30 x 5 = 150
40 x 5 = 200
50 x 5 = 250
60 x 5 = 300
70 x 5 = 350
80 x 5 = 400
90 x 5 = 450
100 x 5 = 500

Example 1:

```
      H | T | O
        | 4 | 2   R 4
  5 ) 2 | 1 | 4
    - 2 | 0 | 0   (40 x 5 = 200)
        | 1 | 4
      - | 1 | 0   (2 x 5 = 10)
        |   | 4
```

Example 2:

```
      H | T | O
        | 6 | 3   R 1
  5 ) 3 | 1 | 6
    - 3 | 0 | 0   (60 x 5 = 300)
        | 1 | 6
      - | 1 | 5   (3 x 5 = 15)
        |   | 1
```

Place Value Division

Directions: Divide. Find the remainder if necessary.

1. T | O

    4) 4 | 9

2. T | O

    3) 5 | 8

3. T | O

    2) 3 | 5

4. T | O

    4) 6 | 5

5. T | O

    5) 7 | 4

6. T | O

    7) 8 | 0

7. T | O

    3) 8 | 4

8. T | O

    6) 7 | 8

9. T | O

    4) 8 | 7

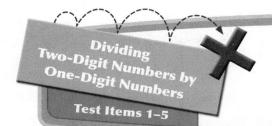

Missing Digit Division

Directions: Look at each division problem. Write the missing digits.

1.
$$9 \overline{)\; 3\,\square} \quad \square\; R\,4$$
$$-\; \square\; 7$$
$$\square$$

2.
$$7 \overline{)\; 4\;\;9} \quad \square$$
$$-\; \square\;\square$$
$$0$$

3.
$$6 \overline{)\; \square\;5} \quad 9\; R\,1$$
$$-\; \square\;\square$$
$$1$$

4.
$$3 \overline{)\; 2\,\square} \quad 6\; R\,2$$
$$-\; \square\; 8$$
$$2$$

5.
$$7 \overline{)\; 1\,\square} \quad 1\; R\,6$$
$$-\; \square$$
$$6$$

6.
$$5 \overline{)\; \square\;3} \quad 6\; R\,\square$$
$$-\; \square\; 0$$
$$\square$$

7.
$$3 \overline{)\; 9\;\;9} \quad \square\; 3$$
$$-\; 9$$
$$\square\; 9$$
$$-\; \square$$
$$0$$

8.
$$2 \overline{)\; \square\;8} \quad 1\;\square$$
$$-\; \square$$
$$0\; 8$$
$$-\; 8$$
$$0$$

9.
$$3 \overline{)\; 2\,\square} \quad 8\; R\,1$$
$$-\; 2\; 4$$
$$\square$$

Two-Digit Division Practice

Directions: Divide to solve each problem.

1. 8)95

2. 9)38

3. 5)14

4. 2)67

5. 7)80

6. 4)29

7. 6)39

8. 6)92

More Two-Digit Division Practice

Directions: Divide to solve each problem.

1. $9\overline{)87}$

2. $5\overline{)23}$

3. $9\overline{)32}$

4. $3\overline{)66}$

5. $2\overline{)81}$

6. $5\overline{)76}$

7. $7\overline{)59}$

8. $3\overline{)37}$

9. $4\overline{)63}$

10. $6\overline{)78}$

11. $6\overline{)59}$

12. $5\overline{)70}$

13. $9\overline{)40}$

14. $4\overline{)82}$

15. $7\overline{)60}$

Three-Digit Division in Place

Dividing Three-Digit Numbers by One-Digit Numbers

Test Items 6–10

Directions: Use place value to help you divide. Some problems may have remainders.

1.   H   T   O

    7) 4   4   8

2.   H   T   O

    6) 4   2   3

3.   H   T   O

    6) 1   1   0

4.   H   T   O

    8) 7   6   2

5.   H   T   O

    6) 4   3   4

6.   H   T   O

    4) 6   5   1

7.   H   T   O

    2) 5   2   8

8.   H   T   O

    6) 3   7   8

Mystery Digits

Directions: Look at each division problem. Write the missing digits.

1.
```
        □ □      R 1
   5 ) 9 1 □
     - 5
       4 1
     - 4 0
         1 □
       - 1 5
           1
```

2.
```
       4 9 9   R 1
   2 ) □ 9 □
       □
     -
       1 9
     - 1 8
       1 □
     - 1 8
```

3.
```
        □ 5   R 1
   8 ) □ 4 □
       □
     -
       0 4
     -   0
         4 1
       - 4 0
           1
```

4.
```
      1 □ □      R 4
   6 ) □
       6      6
     - 6
       □ 1
     -   0
         1 6
       - 1 2
           4
```

5.
```
      □ 3 □
   5 ) 6 9 5
       □
     -
       1 9
     - 1 5
         □ 5
       - 4 5
           0
```

6.
```
        9 □
   7 ) □
       □ 9 3
     - □
       6 3
     - 6 3
         □
```

Three-Digit Division Practice

Dividing Three-Digit Numbers by One-Digit Numbers

Test Items 6–10

Directions: Divide to solve each problem. Some problems may have remainders.

1. 9)126

2. 7)348

3. 9)719

4. 6)444

5. 2)525

6. 6)888

7. 4)821

8. 8)272

9. 6)954

10. 8)522

11. 8)623

12. 4)664

Dividing
Three-Digit Numbers by
One-Digit Numbers

Test Items 6–10

More Three-Digit Division Practice

Directions: Divide to solve each problem. Some problems may have remainders.

1. 7)448

2. 5)348

3. 6)423

4. 4)906

5. 6)110

6. 2)528

7. 7)730

8. 8)768

9. 6)378

10. 8)725

11. 6)434

12. 3)805

End of Book Test

Directions: Read the following problems. Circle the letter beside the correct answer to each question.

Grade Three

1. What number is 10,000 more than **5,328**?

   A. 105,328

   B. 6,328

   C. 15,328

   D. 5,428

2. Subtract. $\begin{array}{r} 500 \\ -231 \\ \hline \end{array}$

   A. 369

   B. 269

   C. 279

   D. 379

3. Add. $\begin{array}{r} 318 \\ +54 \\ \hline \end{array}$

   A. 364

   B. 472

   C. 362

   D. 372

4. Multiply. $7 \times 3 =$ _____

   A. 21

   B. 37

   C. 73

   D. 22

5. Divide. $81 \div 9 =$ _____

   A. 6

   B. 8

   C. 9

   D. 7

6. Multiply. $\begin{array}{r} 63 \\ \times 6 \\ \hline \end{array}$

   A. 369

   B. 2,618

   C. 372

   D. 378

7. Divide. $4\overline{)447}$

   A. 110 R 4

   B. 111 R 3

   C. 112

   D. 111

8. Place the numbers in order from **greatest** to **least**.

   13,322   8,596   19,452   7,570

   A. 13,322 8,596 7,570 19,452

   B. 19,452 13,322 8,596 7,570

   C. 19,452 8,596 13,322 7,570

   D. 19,452 8,596 7,570 13,322

9. Add.   4,613
         + 3,489

   A. 8,102

   B. 8,192

   C. 8,112

   D. 8,122

10. Find the missing number.

    28, 30, _____, 34

    A. 36

    B. 26

    C. 32

    D. 35

11. Subtract.   5,334
              − 1,367

    A. 3,976

    B. 3,961

    C. 4,067

    D. 3,967

12. Divide. $54 \div 6 =$ _____

    A. 9

    B. 8

    C. 6

    D. 10

13. Multiply.   74
              x 5

    A. 360

    B. 720

    C. 370

    D. 350

14. Divide. $6\overline{)48}$

    A. 6

    B. 8

    C. 9

    D. 7

15. Divide.   4)65

  A. 15 R 3

  B. 16

  C. 26

  D. 16 R 1

16. What is the place value of the underlined digit?

34,567

  A. Tens

  B. Ten Thousands

  C. Hundreds

  D. Thousands

17. Add.   5,623
              474
          + 313

  A. 6,410

  B. 5,410

  C. 6,411

  D. 5,411

18. Subtract.   307
              − 39

  A. 278

  B. 268

  C. 262

  D. 272

19. Add.   5 + 5 + 5 + 5 + 5 = _____

  A. 20

  B. 25

  C. 30

  D. 55

20. Divide.   5)35

  A. 9

  B. 6

  C. 8

  D. 7

21. Multiply.   647
               x 9

  A. 5,723

  B. 5,823

  C. 5,813

  D. 5,713

22. Divide.   8)369

  A. 46 R 1

  B. 45 R 6

  C. 46

  D. 44 R 5

23. Write **20 + 500 + 7 + 6,000** in standard form.

    A. 6,525

    B. 6,527

    C. 6,257

    D. 5,627

24. Subtract.
$$\begin{array}{r} 8,457 \\ -\ 4,659 \\ \hline \end{array}$$

    A. 3,708

    B. 3,792

    C. 4,798

    D. 3,798

25. Multiply.   8 x 9 = _____

    A. 72

    B. 89

    C. 98

    D. 74

26. Multiply.
$$\begin{array}{r} 52 \\ \times\ 4 \\ \hline \end{array}$$

    A. 206

    B. 98

    C. 208

    D. 416

27. Divide. $3\overline{)97}$

    A. 32 R 3

    B. 32 R 1

    C. 30 R 2

    D. 31 R 3

28. Multiply.   6 x 9 = _____

    A. 55

    B. 45

    C. 54

    D. 56

29. Multiply.
$$\begin{array}{r} 567 \\ \times\ 4 \\ \hline \end{array}$$

    A. 2,178

    B. 2,168

    C. 2,268

    D. 2,278

30. Divide. $2\overline{)979}$

    A. 369

    B. 489 R 1

    C. 468 R 1

    D. 369 R 1

Answer Key

PAGES 7–8 (DIAGNOSTIC TEST)

1. 5; 2. thousands; 3. 4,321; 4. 7,000; 5. 16,235;
6. 3000 + 400 + 80 + 5; 7. 2,143; 8. 4,438;
9. 10,000 + 3,000 + 800 + 70 + 6; 10. 24,308

PAGE 11

1.

Thousands	Ones
Hundreds:	Hundreds: 5
Tens:	Tens: 4
Ones: 3	Ones: 2

2.

Thousands	Ones
Hundreds:	Hundreds: 6
Tens:	Tens: 5
Ones: 8	Ones: 4

3.

Thousands	Ones
Hundreds:	Hundreds: 7
Tens:	Tens: 8
Ones: 5	Ones: 1

4.

Thousands	Ones
Hundreds:	Hundreds: 5
Tens: 2	Tens: 6
Ones: 1	Ones: 7

5.

Thousands	Ones
Hundreds:	Hundreds: 8
Tens: 1	Tens: 3
Ones: 7	Ones: 4

PAGE 11 (CONTINUED)

6.

Thousands	Ones
Hundreds:	Hundreds: 6
Tens: 3	Tens: 0
Ones: 3	Ones: 3

PAGE 12

1. hundreds, 2. thousands, 3. ones, 4. tens,
5. thousands, 6. hundreds, 7. tens, 8. ones, 9. 4,
10. 4, 11. 7, 12. 5, 13. 6, 14. 4

PAGE 13

1. 745; 2. 8,090; 3. 5,222; 4. 37,251; 5. 14,534;
6. 18,504; 7. 23,716; 8. 10,870; 9. 81,393;
10. 50,641

PAGE 14

1. 3,000 + 200 + 60; 2. 4,000 + 100 + 50;
3. 2,000 + 400 + 70; 4. 5,000 + 300 + 30

PAGE 15

1. 1,000 + 100 + 40 + 6, 1,146, one thousand one
hundred forty-six; 2. 2,000 + 200 + 30 + 6, 2,236,
two thousand two hundred thirty-six; 3. 1,000 + 200
+ 50 + 8, 1,258, one thousand two hundred fifty-eight

PAGE 16

1. 9,000 + 700 + 60 + 3; 2. 8,000 + 100 + 70 + 5;
3. 15,478; 4. 21,699; 5. 10,000 + 800 + 60 + 6;
6. 40,000 + 2,000 + 500 + 80 + 4; 7. 8,547;
8. 9,960; 9. 10,000 + 8,000 + 300 + 50 + 3;
10. 30,000 + 6,000 + 400 + 40 + 4

PAGES 17–18 (DIAGNOSTIC TEST)

1. 4,287; 2. 2,300; 3. 5,542; 4. 2,800, 3,200, 4,500;
5. 256, 2,785, 2,800; 6. <; 7. <; 8. <; 9. >; 10. <

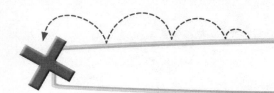

ANSWER KEY

PAGE 23

1. 462; 2. 1,373; 3. 5,420; 4. 16,420; 5. 5,208;
6. 74,437; 7. 10,624; 8. 57,426; 9. 3,233; 10. 39,000

PAGE 24

1. 1,355, 1,356, 1,359, 1,360, 1,361; 2. 5,130, 5,140,
5,160, 5,170, 5,190; 3. 3,300, 3,400, 3,500, 3,700,
3,800; 4. 11,732, 11,752, 11,762, 11,772, 11,792;
5. 8,000, 9,000, 11,000, 12,000, 13,000; 6. 1,545,
7. 3,123; 8. 5,554; 9. 7,800; 10. 4,329; 11. 6,699;
12. 9,980; 13. 3,423; 14. 8,130; 15. 6,601;
16. 4,990; 17. 4,600; 18. 2,216; 19. 9,379; 20. 5,289;
21. 2,460; 22. 7,680; 23. 3,001; 24. 1,765;
25. 5,600; 26. 8,822

PAGE 25

1. 4,200; 2. 4,500; 3. 2,800; 4. 7,200; 5. 3,400;
6. 7,100; 7. 9,200; 8. 8,000; 9. 10,000

PAGE 26

1. 599, 1,350, 5,675, 7,567, 8,590
2. 746, 2,554, 3,453, 6,992, 9,430
3. 19,542, 12,222, 11,703, 8,469, 7,970

PAGE 27

1. >, 2. =, 3. <, 4. =, 5. <, 6. >, 7. >, 8. >, 9. >, 10. >,
11. >, 12. <, 13. <, 14. >, 15. <, 16. <, 17. =, 18. >

PAGES 28–29 (DIAGNOSTIC TEST)

1. 363; 2. 797; 3. 8,092; 4. 4,779; 5. 13,104;
6. 2,700; 7. 6,360; 8. 3,150; 9. 5,411; 10. 1,007

PAGE 33

1. 359; 2. 477; 3. 186; 4. 568; 5. 678; 6. 997; 7. 668;
8. 998; 9. 897; 10. 997; 11. 849; 12. 954; 13. 6,865;
14. 9,387; 15. 7,599; 16. 5,899

PAGE 34

1. 5,083; 2. 6,072; 3. 7,070; 4. 12,700; 5. 9,650;
6. 9,872; 7. 11,930; 8. 7,100; 9. 10,000; 10. 11,950;
11. 7,800; 12. 13,900; 13. 10,135; 14. 10,030;
15. 8,340; 16. 11,144

PAGE 35

1. 3,528; 2. 9,957; 3. 677; 4. 4,500; 5. 3,665;
6. 3,502; 7. 11,612; 8. 2,391; 9. 1,018; 10. 4,703;
11. 7,922; 12. 8,898; 13. 8,189; 14. 5,271; 15. 9,173

PAGE 36

1. 52 + 37 = 89; 2. 457 + 41 = 498; 3. 67 + 32 = 99;
4. 70 + 69 = 139; 5. 573 + 24 = 597; 6. 940 + 40 =
980; 7. 684 + 41 = 725; 8. 887 + 990 = 1,877;
9. 414 + 85 = 499

PAGE 37

1. 267 + 278 = 545; 2. 6,682 + 7,703 = 14,385;
3. 8,713 + 452 = 9,165; 4. 1,601 + 8,525 = 10,126;
5. 1,242 + 339 = 1,581; 6. 4,335 + 5,602 = 9,937

PAGE 38

1. 928; 2. 679; 3. 952; 4. 1,262; 5. 1,001; 6. 1,031;
7. 1,273; 8. 1,197; 9. 749; 10. 635; 11. 1,240;
12. 1,683; 13. 1,009; 14. 607; 15. 1,548; 16. 12,154;
17. 8,618; 18. 10,442; 19. 15,631; 20. 11,042

PAGE 39

1. 4,146; 2. 10,401; 3. 6,336; 4. 3,061; 5. 6,010;
6. 8,763; 7. 4,170; 8. 4,313; 9. 1,321; 10. 5,534;
11. 3,414; 12. 6,044; 13. 4,110; 14. 5,831; 15. 7,412

PAGES 40–41 (DIAGNOSTIC TEST)

1. 3, 30, 300; 2. 10, 100, 1,000; 3. 78; 4. 278;
5. 185; 6. 214; 7. 322; 8. 3,957; 9. 3,171; 10. 2,798

PAGE 47

1. 2, 20, 200; 2. 3, 30, 300; 3. 3, 30, 300; 4. 4, 40,
400, 4,000; 5. 2, 20, 200, 2,000, 20,000; 6. 5, 50,
500; 7. 10, 100, 1,000; 8. 4, 40, 400; 9. 2, 20, 200,
2,000; 10. 5, 50, 500, 5,000

PAGE 48

NUMBER	1 LESS HUNDRED 10 MORE TENS	1 LESS TEN 10 MORE ONES
1. 300	2 10 3̸ 0̸ 0	9 2 1̸0̸ 10 3̸ 0̸ 0
2. 600	5 10 6̸ 0̸ 0	9 5 1̸0̸ 10 6̸ 0̸ 0
3. 304	2 10 3̸ 0̸ 4	9 2 1̸0̸ 14 3̸ 0̸ 4̸
4. 207	1 10 2̸ 0̸ 7	9 1 1̸0̸ 17 2̸ 0̸ 7̸
5. 501	4 10 5̸ 0̸ 1	9 4 1̸0̸ 11 5̸ 0̸ 1̸
6. 403	3 10 4̸ 0̸ 3	9 3 1̸0̸ 13 4̸ 0̸ 3̸
7. 706	6 10 7̸ 0̸ 6	9 6 1̸0̸ 16 7̸ 0̸ 6̸
8. 910	8 11 9̸ 1̸ 0	10 8 1̸1̸ 10 9̸ 1̸ 0̸
9. 800	7 10 8̸ 0̸ 0	9 7 1̸0̸ 10 8̸ 0̸ 0̸
10. 606	5 10 6̸ 0̸ 6	9 5 1̸0̸ 16 6̸ 0̸ 6̸

PAGE 49

1. 272, 2. 155, 3. 131, 4. 49, 5. 345, 6. 116, 7. 55, 8. 169, 9. 111

PAGE 50

1. 87, 2. 88, 3. 98, 4. 192, 5. 108, 6. 509, 7. 290, 8. 129, 9. 308, 10. 466, 11. 102, 12. 277

PAGE 51

1. 1,396; 2. 2,068; 3. 3,148; 4. 4,396; 5. 3,935; 6. 6,922; 7. 3,089; 8. 2,049; 9. 4,278; 10. 3,781; 11. 2,010; 12. 4,704

PAGE 52

1. 35; 2. 4,726; 3. 2,440; 4. 2,590; 5. 2,178; 6. 5,641; 7. 3,994; 8. 2,491; 9. 2,338; 10. 7,755; 11. 3,474; 12. 3,580; 13. 4,569; 14. 2,538; 15. 3,262

PAGE 53

1. 5,985 − 5,462 = 523; 2. 6,927 − 2,215 = 4,712; 3. 9,805 − 6,082 = 3,723; 4. 9,622 − 1,179 = 8,443; 5. 6,223 − 4,723 = 1,500; 6. 8,449 − 8,129 = 320; 7. 5,069 − 3,609 = 1,460; 8. 3,577 − 1,476 = 2,101

PAGES 54–55 (DIAGNOSTIC TEST)

1. 10, 16; 2. 28, 36; 3. 15; 4. 16; 5. 10; 6. 30; 7. 10; 8. 12; 9. 9, 6, 54; 10. 5, 7, 35

PAGE 60

1. 18, 21, 24, 27, 30, 33; 2. 84, 86, 88, 90, 92, 94; 3. 44, 48, 52, 56, 60, 64; 4. 20, 24, 28, 32, 36, 40; 5. 30, 40, 50, 60, 70, 80; 6. 65, 70, 75, 80, 85, 90; 7. 36, 39, 42, 45, 48, 51; 8. 12, 14, 16, 18, 20, 22; 9. 10, 20, 30, 40, 50, 60; 10. 35, 40, 45, 50, 55, 60

PAGE 61

1. 3, 6, 9, 12; 2. 4, 8, 12, 16, 3. 2, 4, 6, 8, 10, 12, 14, 16; 4. 5, 10, 15, 20; 5. 10, 20, 30, 40

PAGE 62

The following numbers should be shaded in each chart: 1. 0, 5, 10, 15, 20, 25, 30, 35, 40; 2. 0, 2, 4, 6, 8, 10, 12, 14, 16, 18, 20, 22, 24, 26, 28, 30, 32, 34, 36, 38, 40, 42, 44; 3. 0, 3, 6, 9, 12, 15, 18, 21, 24, 27, 30, 33, 36, 39, 42; 4. 0, 4, 8, 12, 16, 20, 24, 28, 32, 36, 40, 44; 5. 0, 6, 12, 18, 24, 30, 36, 42; 6. 0, 10, 20, 30, 40; 7. 0, 8, 16, 24, 32, 40; 8. 0, 7, 14, 21, 28, 35, 42

PAGE 63

1. 8, 2. 10, 3. 0, 4. 80, 5. 15, 6. 12, 7. 40, 8. 10, 9. 10, 10. 20, 11. 18, 12. 40, 13. 60, 14. 25, 15. 14, 16. 30, 17. 16, 18. 35, 19. 100, 20. 90

ANSWER KEY

PAGE 64

1. K, 2. G, 3. A, 4. H, 5. I, 6. C, 7. J, 8. E, 9. B, 10. F, 11. L, 12. D

PAGE 65

1. 4 + 4 + 4 = 12, 3 x 4 = 12; 2. 2 + 2 + 2 + 2 = 8, 4 x 2 = 8; 3. 10 + 10 + 10 + 10 = 40, 4 x 10 = 40; 4. 5 + 5 + 5 + 5 + 5 + 5 = 30, 6 x 5 = 30; 5. 2 + 2 + 2 + 2 + 2 = 10, 5 x 2 = 10; 6. 6 + 6 + 6 + 6 = 24, 4 x 6 = 24

PAGE 66

1. 4 + 4 + 4 = 12; 2. 5 + 5 + 5 + 5 = 20; 3. 6 + 6 + 6 = 18; 4. 7 + 7 = 14; 5. 4 + 4 = 8; 6. 3 + 3 + 3 = 9

PAGE 67

1. 4 x 4 = 16; 2. 5 x 3 = 15; 3. 4 x 5 = 20; 4. 2 x 6 = 12

PAGE 68

1. C, 2. F, 3. D, 4. A, 5. B, 6. E, 7. G, 8. H

PAGE 69

1. 3 x 4 = 12, 4 x 3 = 12; 2. 2 x 6 = 12, 6 x 2 = 12; 3. 2 x 4 = 8, 4 x 2 = 8; 4. 2 x 5 = 10, 5 x 2 = 10

PAGES 70–71 (DIAGNOSTIC TEST)

1. 3, 2. 5, 3. 2, 4. 4, 5. 3, 6. 2, 7. 4, 8. 5, 9. 4, 10. 2

PAGE 76

1. 5, 15 ÷ 3 = 5; 2. 2, 8 ÷ 4 = 2; 3. 3, 12 ÷ 4 = 3; 4. 7, 14 ÷ 2 = 7

PAGE 77

1. 4, 12 ÷ 3 = 4; 2. 4, 24 ÷ 6 = 4; 3. 4, 16 ÷ 4 = 4; 4. 6, 30 ÷ 5 = 6; 5. 10, 40 ÷ 4 = 10; 6. 4, 8 ÷ 2 = 4

PAGE 78

1. 4, 20 ÷ 5 = 4; 2. 3, 24 ÷ 8 = 3; 3. 4, 40 ÷ 10 = 4; 4. 6, 36 ÷ 6 = 6; 5. 7, 28 ÷ 4 = 7; 6. 6, 18 ÷ 3 = 6; 7. 5, 20 ÷ 4 = 5; 8. 6, 54 ÷ 9 = 6

PAGE 79

1. 2, 10 ÷ 5 = 2; 2. 3, 12 ÷ 4 = 3; 3. 5, 15 ÷ 3 = 5; 4. 3, 18 ÷ 6 = 3; 5. 5, 20 ÷ 4 = 5; 6. 3, 24 ÷ 8 = 3

PAGE 80

1. 6, 2. 5, 3. 3, 4. 4

PAGE 81

1. 5, 2. 4, 3. 5, 4. 5

PAGE 82

1. 2 x 6 = 12, 6 x 2 = 12, 12 ÷ 2 = 6, 12 ÷ 6 = 2
2. 2 x 4 = 8, 4 x 2 = 8, 8 ÷ 2 = 4, 8 ÷ 4 = 2
3. 2 x 5 = 10, 5 x 2 = 10, 10 ÷ 2 = 5, 10 ÷ 5 = 2
4. 3 x 6 = 18, 6 x 3 = 18, 18 ÷ 3 = 6, 18 ÷ 6 = 3

PAGE 83

Column 1: 1. C, 2. F, 3. I, 4. A, 5. G, 6. D, 7. B, 8. E, 9. J, 10. H
Column 2: 1. d, 2. h, 3. a, 4. g, 5. f, 6. i, 7. c, 8. j, 9. b, 10. e

PAGES 84–85 (DIAGNOSTIC TEST)

1. 10, 2. 12, 3. 18, 4. 30, 5. 32, 6. 36, 7. 42, 8. 48, 9. 81, 10. 90, 11. 8, 12. 14, 13. 15, 14. 24, 15. 28, 16. 25, 17. 36, 18. 54, 19. 72, 20. 7

PAGE 92

1. 8, 2. 18, 3. 8, 4. 18, 5. 6, 6. 16, 7. 6, 8. 16, 9. 4, 10. 14, 11. 12, 12. 2, 13. 2, 14. 0, 15. 10, 16. 20

PAGE 93

1. 20, 2. 45, 3. 20, 4. 45, 5. 15, 6. 40, 7. 15, 8. 40, 9. 10, 10. 35, 11. 30, 12. 5, 13. 5, 14. 0, 15. 25, 16. 50

PAGE 94

1. 5, 2. 35, 3. 15, 4. 30, 5. 10, 6. 20, 7. 40, 8. 45, 9. 50, 10. 20, 11. 25, 12. 0

PAGE 95

1. 5, 50; 2. 3, 30; 3. 8, 80; 4. 4, 40; 5. 0, 0; 6. 2, 20; 7. 6, 60; 8. 7, 70; 9. 1, 10; 10. 10, 100

PAGE 96

1. 20, 2. 80, 3. 30, 4. 10, 5. 80, 6. 0, 7. 70, 8. 90, 9. 40, 10. 100, 11. 60, 12. 50

PAGE 97

1. 6, 2. 24, 3. 3, 4. 15, 5. 21, 6. 0, 7. 12, 8. 9, 9. 30, 10. 18, 11. 27, 12. 24

PAGE 98

1. 4, 2. 28, 3. 12, 4. 24, 5. 8, 6. 16, 7. 32, 8. 36, 9. 40, 10. 28, 11. 20, 12. 0

PAGE 99

1. 6, 2. 42, 3. 18, 4. 36, 5. 12, 6. 24, 7. 48, 8. 54, 9. 60, 10. 42, 11. 30, 12. 0

PAGE 100

1. 7, 2. 28, 3. 21, 4. 42, 5. 14, 6. 35, 7. 56, 8. 63, 9. 70, 10. 49, 11. 35, 12. 0

PAGE 101

1. 8, 2. 56, 3. 24, 4. 48, 5. 16, 6. 32, 7. 64, 8. 72, 9. 80, 10. 56, 11. 40, 12. 0

PAGE 102

1. 9, 2. 36, 3. 27, 4. 54, 5. 18, 6. 45, 7. 72, 8. 81, 9. 90, 10. 63, 11. 45, 12. 0

PAGE 103

1. 18, 2. 4, 3. 6, 4. 16, 5. 14, 6. 2, 7. 8, 8. 20, 9. 0, 10. 12, 11. 18, 12. 20, 13. 4, 14. 10, 15. 6, 16. 8, 17. 12, 18. 16, 19. 14, 20. 20, 21. 8, 22. 2, 23. 12, 24. 14, 25. 16, 26. 0, 27. 6, 28. 18, 29. 12, 30. 6, 31. 10, 32. 16, 33. 18, 34. 14, 35. 8, 36. 4

PAGE 104

1. 27, 2. 9, 3. 6, 4. 24, 5. 21, 6. 3, 7. 12, 8. 24, 9. 0, 10. 18, 11. 6, 12. 30, 13. 6, 14. 15, 15. 9, 16. 12, 17. 18, 18. 24, 19. 21, 20. 30, 21. 0, 22. 3, 23. 18, 24. 21, 25. 24, 26. 18, 27. 9, 28. 27, 29. 18, 30. 9, 31. 15, 32. 24, 33. 27, 34. 21, 35. 12, 36. 6

PAGE 105

1. 36, 2. 8, 3. 12, 4. 32, 5. 28, 6. 4, 7. 16, 8. 32, 9. 0, 10. 24, 11. 8, 12. 40, 13. 16, 14. 20, 15. 12, 16. 8, 17. 24, 18. 32, 19. 28, 20. 40, 21. 16, 22. 4, 23. 24, 24. 28, 25. 32, 26. 24, 27. 12, 28. 36, 29. 24, 30. 12, 31. 20, 32. 32, 33. 36, 34. 28, 35. 16, 36. 8

PAGE 106

1. 45, 2. 10, 3. 15, 4. 40, 5. 35, 6. 5, 7. 20, 8. 40, 9. 0, 10. 30, 11. 10, 12. 50, 13. 20, 14. 25, 15. 15, 16. 10, 17. 30, 18. 40, 19. 35, 20. 50, 21. 20, 22. 5, 23. 30, 24. 35, 25. 40, 26. 0, 27. 15, 28. 45, 29. 30, 30. 15, 31. 25, 32. 40, 33. 45, 34. 35, 35. 20, 36. 10

PAGE 107

1. 54, 2. 12, 3. 18, 4. 48, 5. 42, 6. 6, 7. 24, 8. 48, 9. 0, 10. 36, 11. 12, 12. 60, 13. 24, 14. 30, 15. 18, 16. 12, 17. 36, 18. 48, 19. 42, 20. 60, 21. 24, 22. 6, 23. 36, 24. 42, 25. 48, 26. 0, 27. 18, 28. 54, 29. 36, 30. 18, 31. 30, 32. 48, 33. 54, 34. 42, 35. 24, 36. 12

PAGE 108

1. 63, 2. 14, 3. 21, 4. 56, 5. 49, 6. 7, 7. 28, 8. 56, 9. 0, 10. 42, 11. 14, 12. 70, 13. 28, 14. 35, 15. 21, 16. 14, 17. 42, 18. 56, 19. 49, 20. 70, 21. 28, 22. 7, 23. 42, 24. 49, 25. 56, 26. 0, 27. 21, 28. 63, 29. 42, 30. 21, 31. 35, 32. 56, 33. 63, 34. 49, 35. 28, 36. 14

PAGE 109

1. 72, 2. 16, 3. 24, 4. 64, 5. 56, 6. 8, 7. 32, 8. 64, 9. 0, 10. 48, 11. 16, 12. 80, 13. 32, 14. 40, 15. 24, 16. 16, 17. 48, 18. 64, 19. 56, 20. 80, 21. 32, 22. 8, 23. 48, 24. 56, 25. 64, 26. 0, 27. 24, 28. 72, 29. 48, 30. 24, 31. 40, 32. 64, 33. 72, 34. 56, 35. 32, 36. 16

PAGE 110

1. 81, 2. 18, 3. 27, 4. 72, 5. 63, 6. 9, 7. 36, 8. 72, 9. 0, 10. 54, 11. 18, 12. 90, 13. 36, 14. 45, 15. 27, 16. 18, 17. 54, 18. 72, 19. 63, 20. 90, 21. 36, 22. 9, 23. 54, 24. 63, 25. 72, 26. 0, 27. 27, 28. 81, 29. 54, 30. 27, 31. 45, 32. 72, 33. 81, 34. 63, 35. 36, 36. 18

PAGE 111

1. 72, 2. 12, 3. 4, 4. 40, 5. 27, 6. 15, 7. 60, 8. 14, 9. 28, 10. 6, 11. 14, 12. 48, 13. 49, 14. 0, 15. 32, 16. 40, 17. 9, 18. 6, 19. 25, 20. 18, 21. 20, 22. 21, 23. 2, 24. 42, 25. 72, 26. 8, 27. 12, 28. 81, 29. 18, 30. 18, 31. 25, 32. 32, 33. 18, 34. 7, 35. 0, 36. 16

PAGE 112

1. 27, 2. 6, 3. 20, 4. 64, 5. 0, 6. 45, 7. 70, 8. 12, 9. 21, 10. 5, 11. 28, 12. 54, 13. 49, 14. 2, 15. 40, 16. 90, 17. 72, 18. 21, 19. 24, 20. 24, 21. 30, 22. 32, 23. 6, 24. 56, 25. 63, 26. 18, 27. 20, 28. 81, 29. 28, 30. 21, 31. 36, 32. 45, 33. 0, 34. 16, 35. 0, 36. 18

PAGES 113–114 (DIAGNOSTIC TEST)

1. 2, 2. 4, 3. 6, 4. 9, 5. 6, 6. 7, 7. 9, 8. 9, 9. 9, 10. 0, 11. 9, 12. 7, 13. 5, 14. 8, 15. 9

PAGE 120

1. 4, 2. 9, 3. 8, 4. 3, 5. 2, 6. 7, 7. 6, 8. 1, 9. 5, 10. 0

PAGE 121

1. 2, 2. 5, 3. 8, 4. 1, 5. 3, 6. 4, 7. 0, 8. 6, 9. 10, 10. 9

PAGE 122

1. 7, 2. 7, 3. 8, 4. 8, 5. 4, 6. 4, 7. 9, 8. 9, 9. 8, 10. 8, 11. 4, 12. 4

PAGE 123

Circled numbers: 99, 96, 93, 90, 87, 84, 81, 78, 75, 72, 69, 66, 63, 60, 57, 54, 51, 48, 45, 42, 39, 36, 33, 30, 27, 24, 21, 18, 15, 12, 9, 6, 3

1. 9, 2. 4, 3. 5, 4. 3, 5. 2, 6. 7, 7. 1, 8. 6, 9. 8, 10. 0

PAGE 124

Circled numbers: 100, 96, 92, 88, 84, 80, 76, 72, 68, 64, 60, 56, 52, 48, 44, 40, 36, 32, 28, 24, 20, 16, 12, 8, 4

1. 7, 2. 3, 3. 6, 4. 2, 5. 1, 6. 8, 7. 0, 8. 5, 9. 9, 10. 4

PAGE 125

1. $24 \div 3 = 8$, 2. $27 \div 3 = 9$, 3. $9 \div 3 = 3$, 4. $21 \div 3 = 7$

PAGE 126

1. $24 \div 4 = 6$, 2. $28 \div 4 = 7$, 3. $16 \div 4 = 4$, 4. $20 \div 4 = 5$

PAGE 127

1. $42 \div 6 = 7$, $42 \div 7 = 6$; 2. $14 \div 2 = 7$, $14 \div 7 = 2$; 3. $18 \div 6 = 3$, $18 \div 3 = 6$; 4. $56 \div 8 = 7$, $56 \div 7 = 8$; 5. $35 \div 5 = 7$, $35 \div 7 = 5$; 6. $54 \div 6 = 9$, $54 \div 9 = 6$; 7. $48 \div 8 = 6$, $48 \div 6 = 8$; 8. $56 \div 8 = 7$, $56 \div 7 = 8$; 9. $30 \div 6 = 5$, $30 \div 5 = 6$; 10. $24 \div 6 = 4$, $24 \div 4 = 6$; 11. $21 \div 3 = 7$, $21 \div 7 = 3$; 12. $63 \div 9 = 7$, $63 \div 7 = 9$

PAGE 128

1. 3, 2, 5; 2. 3, 5, 1; 3. 1, 6, 8; 4. 9, 1, 8; 5. 10, 5, 2; 6. 6, 3, 7; 7. 9, 7, 1; 8. 2, 5, 10; 9. 10, 3, 5; 10. 3, 9, 4

PAGE 129

1. $40 \div 8 = 5$, $40 \div 5 = 8$; 2. $54 \div 6 = 9$, $54 \div 9 = 6$; 3. $56 \div 8 = 7$, $56 \div 7 = 8$; 4. $45 \div 5 = 9$, $45 \div 9 = 5$; 5. $48 \div 8 = 6$, $48 \div 6 = 8$; 6. $27 \div 9 = 3$, $27 \div 3 = 9$; 7. $36 \div 4 = 9$, $36 \div 9 = 4$; 8. $32 \div 8 = 4$, $32 \div 4 = 8$; 9. $72 \div 8 = 9$, $72 \div 9 = 8$; 10. $24 \div 3 = 8$, $24 \div 8 = 3$; 11. $16 \div 8 = 2$, $16 \div 2 = 8$; 12. $80 \div 10 = 8$, $80 \div 8 = 10$

PAGE 130

1. 3, 2, 6; 2. 5, 2, 1; 3. 8, 4, 1; 4. 6, 7, 3; 5. 9, 7, 5; 6. 5, 6, 9; 7. 1, 2, 6; 8. 8, 0, 4; 9. 7, 9, 8; 10. 9, 2, 1

PAGE 131

1. 9, 2. 0, 3. 9, 4. 5, 5. 5, 6. 1, 7. 8, 8. 10, 9. 3, 10. 7, 11. 2, 12. 9, 13. 1, 14. 6, 15. 1, 16. 9, 17. 10, 18. 9, 19. 6, 20. 3, 21. 5, 22. 8, 23. 8, 24. 8, 25. 5, 26. 12, 27. 6, 28. 1

PAGE 132

1. 2, 2. 2, 3. 2, 4. 0, 5. 4, 6. 5, 7. 5, 8. 5, 9. 6, 10. 6, 11. 6, 12. 7, 13. 7, 14. 7, 15. 1, 16. 0, 17. 8, 18. 8, 19. 6, 20. 6, 21. 5, 22. 6, 23. 4, 24. 2, 25. 8, 26. 2, 27. 1, 28. 9

PAGE 133

1. 5, 2. 1, 3. 9, 4. 0, 5. 6, 6. 2, 7. 6, 8. 7, 9. 2, 10. 2, 11. 3, 12. 7, 13. 7, 14. 4, 15. 0, 16. 9, 17. 3, 18. 2, 19. 5, 20. 9, 21. 7, 22. 8, 23. 5, 24. 4, 25. 7, 26. 1, 27. 8, 28. 8

PAGE 134

1. 8, 2. 7, 3. 2, 4. 6, 5. 5, 6. 3, 7. 9, 8. 7, 9. 2, 10. 4, 11. 7, 12. 9, 13. 6, 14. 3, 15. 3, 16. 6, 17. 9, 18. 5, 19. 6, 20. 4, 21. 2, 22. 8, 23. 7, 24. 5, 25. 2, 26. 8, 27. 8, 28. 3

PAGE 135

1. 2, 2. 6, 3. 8, 4. 7, 5. 7, 6. 7, 7. 8, 8. 4, 9. 3, 10. 6, 11. 8, 12. 1, 13. 8, 14. 9, 15. 9, 16. 9, 17. 4, 18. 5, 19. 3, 20. 5, 21. 2, 22. 3, 23. 6, 24. 5, 25. 9, 26. 8, 27. 8, 28. 4

PAGE 136

1. 2, 2. 6, 3. 5, 4. 4, 5. 7, 6. 9, 7. 3, 8. 8, 9. 10, 10. 6, 11. 9, 12. 2, 13. 8, 14. 9, 15. 1, 16. 4, 17. 4, 18. 6, 19. 7, 20. 3, 21. 5, 22. 2, 23. 8, 24. 3, 25. 2, 26. 2, 27. 7, 28. 9

PAGE 137

1. 2, 2. 9, 3. 5, 4. 6, 5. 4, 6. 3, 7. 1, 8. 8, 9. 6, 10. 7, 11. 4, 12. 5, 13. 8, 14. 8, 15. 7, 16. 9, 17. 5, 18. 3, 19. 4, 20. 2, 21. 2, 22. 3, 23. 8, 24. 7, 25. 5, 26. 5, 27. 4, 28. 9

PAGE 138

1. 2, 2. 2, 3. 16, 4. 6, 5. 24, 6. 9, 7. 5, 8. 7, 9. 9, 10. 27, 11. 6, 12. 8, 13. 8, 14. 25, 15. 2, 16. 18, 17. 4, 18. 4, 19. 8, 20. 5, 21. 9, 22. 56, 23. 45, 24. 6, 25. 24, 26. 6, 27. 8, 28. 5

PAGES 139–140 (DIAGNOSTIC TEST)

1. 4 x 11; 2. 4 x 12; 3. 5 x 21; 4. 6 x 25 = 150; 5. 3 x 32 = 96; 6. 144; 7. 42; 8. 80; 9. 1,452; 10. 2,106

PAGE 147

1. 5 x 21 = 105; 2. 3 x 32 = 96; 3. 4 x 11 = 44; 4. 4 x 12 = 48; 5. 3 x 42 = 126; 6. 4 x 31 = 124; 7. 4 x 23 = 92; 8. 4 x 41 = 164

PAGE 148

1. 4 x 22 = 88; 2. 3 x 42 = 126; 3. 3 x 14 = 42; 4. 4 x 32 = 128; 5. 3 x 43 = 129; 6. 3 x 51 = 153; 7. 3 x 23 = 69; 8. 3 x 62 = 186

PAGE 149

1. 4 x 32 = 128, 2. 3 x 44 = 132, 3. 3 x 15 = 45, 4. 3 x 24 = 72, 5. 3 x 53 = 159, 6. 3 x 52 = 156, 7. 4 x 22 = 88, 8. 3 x 63 = 189

PAGE 150

1. 46, (2 x 20) + (2 x 3), Model: || || + ••• •••, Regroup: not needed, Add: 4 tens + 6 ones = 46
2. 136, (4 x 30) + (4 x 4), Model: ||| ||| ||| ||| + •••• •••• •••• ••••; Regroup: ||| ||| ||| ||| | + ••• •••, Add: 13 tens + 6 ones = 136
3. 63, (3 x 20) + (3 x 1), Model: || || || + •••, Regroup: not needed, Add: 6 tens + 3 ones = 63
4. 57, (3 x 10) + (3 x 9), Model: | | | + ••••••••• ••••••••• •••••••••, Regroup: ||||| + •••••••, Add: 5 tens + 7 ones = 57

PAGE 151

1. 36, (2 x 10) + (2 x 8), Model: || + •••••••• ••••••••, Regroup: ||| + ••••••, Add: 3 tens + 6 ones = 36
2. 132, (3 x 40) + (3 x 4), Model: |||| |||| |||| + •••• •••• ••••, Regroup: |||| |||| |||| | + ••, Add: 13 tens + 2 ones = 132
3. 88, (4 x 20) + (4 x 2), Model: || || || || + •• •• •• ••, Regroup: not needed, Add: 8 tens + 8 ones = 88
4. 58, (2 x 20) + (2 x 9), Model: || || + ••••••••• •••••••••, Regroup: || || | + •••• ••••, Add: 5 tens + 8 ones = 58

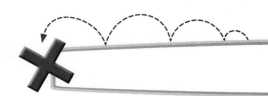

PAGE 152

1. 100, Model: || || || || + ••••• ••••• •••••
••••• , Regroup: || || || || ||, Add: 10 tens = 100,
Partial Product: 25 x 4 = 20 + 80 = 100
2. 205, |||| |||| |||| |||| |||| + •••••, Regroup: not
needed, Add: 20 tens + 5 ones = 205, Partial
Product: 41 x 5 = 5 + 200 = 205
3. 192, ||| ||| ||| ||| ||| ||| + •• •• •• •• •• ••,
Regroup: ||| ||| ||| ||| ||| ||| | + ••, Add: 19 tens + 2
ones = 192, Partial Product: 32 x 6 = 12 + 180 = 192

PAGE 153

1. 162, 2. 140, 3. 172, 4. 280, 5. 208, 6. 192, 7. 216,
8. 558, 9. 164, 10. 273, 11. 235, 12. 370

PAGE 154

1. 84, 2. 196, 3. 336, 4. 752, 5. 216, 6. 512, 7. 355,
8. 222, 9. 255, 10. 246, 11. 200, 12. 485

PAGE 155

1. 801, 2. 161, 3. 420, 4. 196, 5. 608, 6. 144, 7. 90,
8. 295, 9. 336, 10. 468, 11. 265, 12. 385, 13. 588,
14. 576, 15. 111, 16. 360

PAGE 156

1. 312, 2. 252, 3. 158, 4. 430, 5. 237, 6. 420, 7. 576,
8. 378, 9. 760, 10. 423, 11. 114, 12. 192, 13. 616,
14. 440, 15. 112, 16. 486

PAGE 157

1. 76, 2. 235, 3. 129, 4. 413, 5. 558, 6. 344, 7. 128,
8. 300, 9. 170, 10. 164, 11. 432, 12. 364, 13. 340,
14. 175, 15. 348

PAGE 158

1. 335, 2. 168, 3. 828, 4. 238, 5. 405, 6. 360,
7. 266, 8. 402, 9. 198, 10. 164, 11. 588, 12. 576,
13. 111, 14. 282, 15. 285

PAGE 159

1. 95, 2. 432, 3. 372, 4. 312, 5. 252, 6. 632, 7. 567,
8. 430, 9. 237, 10. 504, 11. 348, 12. 648, 13. 350,
14. 378, 15. 469

PAGE 160

1. 3,055; 2. 3,544; 3. 528; 4. 5,100; 5. 3,170;
6. 3,488; 7. 1,764; 8. 5,635; 9. 405; 10. 2,748;
11. 3,835; 12. 1,696; 13. 2,505; 14. 2,700; 15. 1,305

PAGE 161

1. 2,379; 2. 3,912; 3. 3,752; 4. 2,716; 5. 783,
6. 1,930; 7. 1,437; 8. 4,088; 9. 852, 10. 7,776;
11. 2,610; 12. 3,978; 13. 2,268; 14. 3,960; 15. 5,823

PAGE 162

1. 3,925; 2. 3,092; 3. 5,106; 4. 4,446; 5. 2,262;
6. 1,808; 7. 4,485; 8. 668; 9. 1,477; 10. 1,688;
11. 2,205; 12. 4,272; 13. 872; 14. 4,650; 15. 3560

PAGE 163

1. 1,935; 2. 1,416; 3. 1,912; 4. 2,910; 5. 1,791;
6. 3,108; 7. 8,685; 8. 1,904; 9. 6,671; 10. 819;
11. 4,680; 12. 1,470; 13. 1,530; 14. 3,828; 15. 3,498

PAGE 164

1. 1,676; 2. 2,735; 3. 1,929; 4. 2,513; 5. 2,358;
6. 6,744; 7. 3,728; 8. 2,700; 9. 3,170; 10. 1,364;
11. 4,632; 12. 4,564; 13. 3,140; 14. 4,675; 15. 1,948

PAGE 165

1. 1,095; 2. 2,832; 3. 2,772; 4. 5,112; 5. 952;
6. 3,032; 7. 5,067; 8. 3,930; 9. 2,937; 10. 1,704;
11. 1,948; 12. 6,048; 13. 3,850; 14. 3,378; 15. 2,569

PAGES 166–167 (DIAGNOSTIC TEST)

1. 100; 2. 10; 3. 30; 4. 6; 5. 6; 6. 6, 0; 7. 4, 4; 8. 7,
1; 9. 15 R 3; 10. 10 R 4

PAGE 174

1. 100; 2. 100; 3. 20, 200; 4. 3, 900; 5. 20, 400, 200; 6. 20, 200; 7. 2, 20, 20; 8. 3, 30, 600; 9. 5, 100, 5; 10. 3, 3, 400

PAGE 175

1. 12, 3, 4, 4; 2. 18, 3, 6, 6; 3. 15, 3, 5, 5; 4. 4; 5. 3; 6. 4; 7. 7 x 3 = 21; 21 ÷ 3 = 7

PAGE 176

1. D, 2; 2. E, 6; 3. B, 6; 4. C, 3; 5. A, 8; 6. F, 7

PAGE 177

1. 9, 2. 1, 3. 5, 4. 5, 5. 4, 6. 15, 7. 8, 8. 15

PAGE 178

1. 6, 2. 8, 3. 6, 4. 28, 5. 12, 6. 9

PAGE 179

1. 4, 2. 5, 3. 4, 4. 5, 5. 5, 6. 7, 7. 6, 8. 7, 9. 8, 10. 9, 11. 8, 12. 6, 13. 7, 14. 8, 15. 9, 16. 9

PAGE 180

1. 23 R 1, 2. 17 R 1, 3. 16 R 1, 4. 4 R 4, 5. 4 R 3, 6. 3 R 3, 7. 14 R 4, 8. 10 R 3, 9. 8 R 3, 10. 12 R 3, 11. 6 R 1, 12. 7 R 2, 13. 11 R 1, 14. 11 R 1, 15. 12 R 3, 16. 9 R 4

PAGE 181

1. 9 R 3, 2. 5 R 3, 3. 5 R 3, 4. 6 R 3, 5. 5 R 2, 6. 6 R 6, 7. 7 R 4, 8. 16 R 1, 9. 9 R 3, 10. 10 R 7, 11. 6 R 6, 12. 5 R 2, 13. 10 R 8, 14. 4 R 3, 15. 12 R 4, 16. 12 R 2

PAGES 182–183 (DIAGNOSTIC TEST)

1. 14 R 3, 2. 32 R 1, 3. 11 R 4, 4. 16 R 1, 5. 9 R 4, 6. 59, 7. 46 R 1, 8. 98 R 6, 9. 111 R 3, 10. 469 R 1

PAGE 187

1. 12 R 1, 2. 19 R 1, 3. 17 R 1, 4. 16 R 1, 5. 14 R 4, 6. 11 R 3, 7. 28, 8. 13, 9. 21 R 3

PAGE 188

From top to bottom, read left to right:
1. 3, 1, 2, 4; 2. 7, 4, 9; 3. 5, 5, 4; 4. 0, 1; 5. 3, 7; 6. 3, 3, 3, 3; 7. 3, 0, 9; 8. 4, 2, 2; 9. 5, 1

PAGE 189

1. 11 R 7, 2. 4 R 2, 3. 2 R 4, 4. 33 R 1, 5. 11 R 3, 6. 7 R 1, 7. 6 R 3, 8. 15 R 2

PAGE 190

1. 9 R 6, 2. 4 R 3, 3. 3 R 5, 4. 22, 5. 40 R 1, 6. 15 R 1, 7. 8 R 3, 8. 12 R 1, 9. 15 R 3, 10. 13, 11. 9 R 5, 12. 14, 13. 4 R 4, 14. 20 R 2, 15. 8 R 4

PAGE 191

1. 64, 2. 70 R 3, 3. 18 R 2, 4. 95 R 2, 5. 72 R 2, 6. 162 R 3, 7. 264, 8. 63

PAGE 192

From top to bottom, read left to right:
1. 8, 3, 6, 6; 2. 9, 9, 8, 9; 3. 0, 8, 1, 8; 4. 0, 2, 1, 0; 5. 1, 9, 5, 4; 6. 9, 6, 6, 0

PAGE 193

1. 14, 2. 49 R 5, 3. 79 R 8, 4. 74, 5. 262 R 1, 6. 148, 7. 205 R 1, 8. 34, 9. 159, 10. 65 R 2, 11. 77 R 7, 12. 166

PAGE 194

1. 64, 2. 69 R 3, 3. 70 R 3, 4. 226 R 2, 5. 18 R 2, 6. 264, 7. 104 R 2, 8. 96, 9. 63, 10. 90 R 5, 11. 72 R 2, 12. 268 R 1

PAGES 195–198 (END OF BOOK TEST)

1. C, 2. B, 3. D, 4. A, 5. C, 6. D, 7. B, 8. B, 9. A, 10. C, 11. D, 12. A, 13. C, 14. B, 15. D, 16. D, 17. A, 18. B, 19. B, 20. D, 21. B, 22. A, 23. B, 24. D, 25. A, 26. C, 27. B, 28. C, 29. C, 30. B

Certificate

OF COMPLETION

This is to certify that

_____

has completed the mathematics exercises in

Jump Into Math!

Grade 3

_____
SCHOOL

_____
TEACHER'S SIGNATURE

_____
DATE